DRAGONS
TOUCH

WEAKNESSES OF THE
HUMAN ANATOMY

DRAGONS TOUCH

MASTER HEI LONG

PALADIN PRESS
BOULDER,COLORADO

Also by Master Hei Long:

Advanced Dragon's Touch: 20 Anatomical Targets and
  Techniques for Taking Them Out

Da Zhimingde: Striking Deadly Blows to Vital Organs

Danger Zones: Defending Yourself against Surprise Attack

Gouzao Gonji: Seven Neurological Attacks for Inflicting
  Serious Damage

Guge Gongji: Seven Primary Targets to Take Anyone Out of a
  Fight

Iron Hand of the Dragon's Touch: Secrets of Breaking Power

Master's Guide to Basic Self-Defense: Progressive Retraining
  of the Reflexive Response

Dragons Death Touch: Weaknesses of the Human Anatomy
by Master Hei Long
Copyright © 1983 by Master Hei Long

ISBN 0-87364-271-6
Printed in the United States of America

Published by Paladin Press, a division of
Paladin Enterprises, Inc., P.O. Box 1307,
Boulder, Colorado 80306, USA.
(303) 443-7250

Direct inquiries and/or orders to the above address.

PALADIN, PALADIN PRESS, and the "horse head" design
are trademarks belonging to Paladin Enterprises and
registered in United States Patent and Trademark Office.

Visit our Web site at www.paladin-press.com

Contents

Warning

Some of the techniques depicted in this book are extremely dangerous. It is not the intent of the author, publisher, or distributors of this book to encourage readers to attempt any of these techniques without proper professional supervison and training. Attempting to do so can result in serious injury or death. Do not attempt any of these techniques without the supervision of a certified instructor.

The author, publisher, and distributors of this book disclaim any liability from any damages or injuries of any type that a reader or user of information contained herein may encounter from the use or misuse of said information. *This book is presented for academic study only.*

Preface

What are the martial arts? A religion, or a part of a religion; a way of life; a form of artful expression; a skill of mind or body, or both; the scientific development of combative skills? All of the above? Perhaps. It depends upon the school where you teach or study. Today, the majority of martial arts schools available to the public are designed for and operated by the financial machine known as free enterprise—the American capitalist way. A student is a fee, a test is a fee, rank is a fee. Demonstrations? I can only shake my head in disgust. I once saw a master fall into a set of ring ropes and onto his can after throwing an aerial side kick that was off-focus at least eight inches, resulting in his entanglement in the ropes. That same master operates a successful school of about two hundred students. I have seen black belts from this school that could not throw an even remotely proper side kick. It is true, we all must survive, so we sell our knowledge to those who dare venture into the world of martial arts. But to give rank to an undeserving student is dishonorable. Perhaps tomorrow the world we live in will demand honor and respect for all martial artists, students as well as instructors.

The contents of this book represent my first contribution to all of America's martial artists. It was not intended to be a book, and was certainly not meant to be taught to students outside the Lian Shi system of Kung Fu. The information laid out here was given to me by my second instructor, a master of Lian Shi, about seventeen years ago. The material has been edited and updated but is almost entirely original. It was put into book form to allow one of my stress points in teaching to reach the minds of serious martial artists whom I will never meet. It is my belief as a practical man and a sincere instructor that knowledge of body weaknesses is every bit as important as the ability to hit a given target proficiently. A defense situation may arise in which hitting conventional targets does not stop the attacker. I have taught many young women, and I could not sleep at night if I told a four-foot-eleven-inch girl of ninety-two pounds that a kick in the groin and a combination punch to the face is going to stop a six-foot-four-inch, two-hundred-and-forty-pound weight lifter. It would be unfair, dishonorable, and disrespectful to myself and to the student. On the other hand, a forefist strike to the anterior neck region, followed by a claw strike to the eyes and a horizontal forearm strike to the carotid plexus with full hip rotation would do the job if properly executed. Yes, a scientific attack using the knowledge of anatomical human torso weaknesses. A brutal and crippling combination, likely to be fatal. A deadly set of movements that could keep your daughter or wife from being raped or beaten—or both. The techniques presented here are designed to keep you alive—the survivor instead of the victim.

The knowledge of where to hit, coupled with technique, is indeed devastating. Such knowledge and technique should be part of the training of every martial artist, reaffirming the once commonplace assumption that a martial arts fighter can be deadly. Somewhere, somehow, as the martial arts evolved in the United

States, some profiteering ideologist infected the very heart of the purpose of martial arts and made it a sport, like boxing. Today there are prizes, trophies, and national recognition for competition fighters. To watch them fight is no different than watching boxing matches. You will not find this infection in Lian Shi Kung Fu.

The knowledge of where to hit is not enough. There are many factors involved in training to attack anatomical targets. But as the initial step, *where* is the question that is answered here.

If you have taken the time to read this introduction, I hope my words have conveyed my sincerity, and that these words encourage you to study this book, not just read it.

Tsung chin ou shau chi chhi shau yee.
"With respect to my school and what it represents."

Introduction

As you read on and begin the anatomy study, you will find that there are forty-three pressure points cited as target areas. Other areas of the body sensitive to attack have not been listed in this text. Why these forty-three? Because they are the most practical with all factors considered in each of the five chapters. To illustrate two hundred pressure points would be futile for an effective analysis. It would turn a logically prepared study into a wasteful collection of printed matter. If you cannot hit one of the forty-three named target areas in a given situation, you could not hit a hundred more if you knew them. The most crucial targets are of course included in this work; no major pressure point has been omitted. With the knowledge gained from this book, a sincere martial artist would in fact be deadly at his or her will, but only if the study contained here were incorporated into regular training sessions and properly practiced. The knowledge is here; gain it! Add it to your martial arts arsenal. Achieve the ability to use the knowledge and your body will have the power of causing death. But remember: a force exists in the universe that balances all things in life. Some refer to it as God, a supreme being. Some call it Karma. It has many names, but it does exist. Always be just. If you are taking a life because it is necessary defensively to pre-

serve your life or the life of a loved one, or that life is
being taken as just reciprocation for an evil deed, then
the Universal Force, I believe, will not take vengeance.
However, if you unjustly take a life, you will reap the
vengeance of the Universal Force, perhaps not with your
life but with the life of one you love, or with all that
you live for. A man can die many times in his life. This
is the philosophy of Lian Shi.

With this knowledge, gain power over yourself, and
with practice and study, achieve power over your
enemies.

It should be understood that the contents of this
book are the anatomical studies taught as the theory
and philosophy governing the practice of focus and intended mastery of Lian Shi Kung Fu. The illustrations
are not scaled and are in some cases exaggerated to
ensure understanding of the subject target and should
not be used for or relied on for any purpose other than
the study of Lian Shi.

Pressure Point Classifications

Numerical

I	Brain or skull
II	Sense organs
III	Life support, cardiorespiratory, major organs and tracts
IV	Muscular functions and nerves
V	Mechanical functions, skeletal, cartilages and joints

Alphabetical

A	Immobility from pain
B	Immobility from structural or organic damage
C	Unconsciousness from nerve or organic damage
D	Death from any physiological damage

Meaning and Purpose

Each target is classified in numerical (anatomical representation) and alphabetical (physical reaction) figures. For example, pressure point 14 would be III for life support, cardiorespiratory, major organs and tracts, and D for death from physiological damage. Pressure point 14 is a III-D class target area. Pressure point 39 would be a V-B class target. The numerals tell you what basic physiological function is performed by the target, and the letters tell you what physical reaction to expect. It is wise to know the results of your strike as well as the location of the target.

Striking force is critical in attacking pressure points, as it will determine the resulting damage. For example, pressure point 30, the abdominal area, is classified III-B. The B suggests that immobility from structural or organic damage could occur as the result of effectively attacking the umbilicus. This is true, but only with sufficient striking force. A less powerful strike could mean an A class result, or no reaction at all. The term *sufficient force* will be used many times in Chapter 3. What is sufficient force? The question is difficult. It would, of course, take less power to cause hernia to the aponeurosis around the umbilicus (see pressure point 30) of a twenty-five-year-old man who gets drunk three times a week and forgot what a sit-up was after high school than a man of the same age that weight trains or trains in martial arts regularly. After thinking it through thoroughly, it was determined that far too many factors were involved to apply an even remotely accurate weight force to a target to effect a specific amount of damage. Therefore, the term *sufficient force* for the purpose of this text means a firmly massed power focused with six to twelve inches of snap penetration for arm strikes, and twelve to twenty-four inches of penetration for leg strikes. The techniques illustrated in Chapter 4 give a basic concept of penetration, which is an absolute necessity in applying sufficient force.

1. Dragons Strike to the Head

The ventral transverse plane is comprised of the face, the front, top and sides of the head, the neck, and the upper torso, including the collarbone. There are a total of fifteen pressure points in this chapter.

1. Coronal suture
2. Trigeminal nerve and frontal bone
3. Temple and fossa temporalis
4. Eyes
5. Ears
6. Mastoid
7. Septal cartilage
8. Anterior nasal spine
9. Temporomandibular joint
10. Tip of the mandible
11. Sternocleidomastoid region
12. Anterior neck region
13. Brachial plexus and trapezius muscle
14. Suprasternal notch
15. Clavicle bone

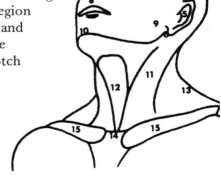

Coronal Suture

The coronal suture is the joint of the two frontal and parietal bones of the cranium (figure 1). The joint extends from temple to temple across the frontal portion of the skull (figure 2). At the centermost point of the coronal suture and extending slightly to the front is the area known as the anterolateral fontanel (figure 3). The space between the bones exists as membrane at birth and closes up within eighteen months. Although fusion is generally complete after two years, the coronal suture remains weaker than the rest of the skull.

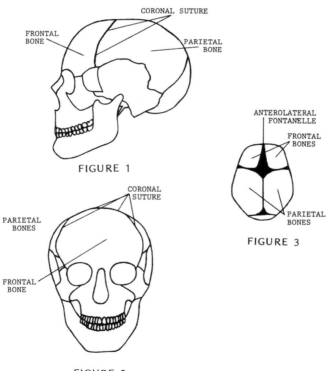

FIGURE 1

FIGURE 3

FIGURE 2

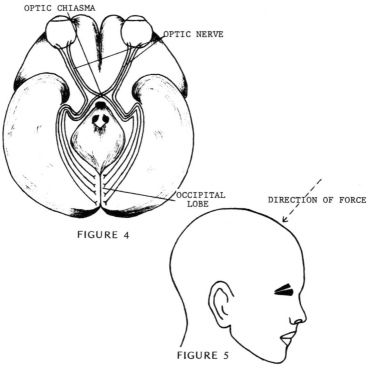

OPTIC CHIASMA

OPTIC NERVE

OCCIPITAL
LOBE

DIRECTION OF FORCE

FIGURE 4

FIGURE 5

Directly beneath this pressure point is the brain area known as the sensory motor, which controls articulation of the legs, arms, hands, and lips. Deep within the brain under this area is the optic chiasma, the crossing of the optic nerves on their way to the occipital lobe at the cerebral portion of the skull (figure 4). A strike to the coronal suture, depending on the impact, could cause concussion, temporary blindness, unconsciousness, brain hemorrhage, and if an extremely powerful blow is delivered, death. With the proper pressure, severing of the joint is possible. Figure 5 shows the preferred direction in which force should be applied. The coronal suture is a class I-C target area.

Master Long has taken a defensive position against his opponent.

Opponent slides forward and attempts a low reverse punch. Master Long drops his elbow in a 45 degree block while cocking the hammer strike to follow and also cocking the hips.

In his final movement, the counterattack is delivered with a full overhead hammer strike to the anterolateral fontanel, or coronal suture. The hips, shoulder and stance have fully rotated with the flow of force to ensure that the maximum amount of pressure is given to the strike.

Frontal Bone and Trigeminal Nerve

The frontal bone and trigeminal nerve can be struck simultaneously just below the centermost point of the forehead (figure 6). Note also that the facial nerve crosses this area. Figures 7 and 8 depict the nerve origins and branches. Because the nerves are on the exterior of the skull, striking the frontal bone will trap the nerves between the contact point of the anatomical weapon and the frontal portion of the skull, making this attack easily effective with sufficient pressure. Impact on the frontal bone could result in jarring of the cerebral hemispheres located in the rear portion of the brain (figure 9). Unconsciousness and concussion could result. Impaired vision and paralysis (temporary or permanent) could occur from a reaction of the additional branches of the facial and trigeminal nerves. Whiplash could occur, and if maximum impact is applied, death could easily result from brain hemorrhage. This is a class I-D target area. Figure 10 shows the proper angle at which to apply force.

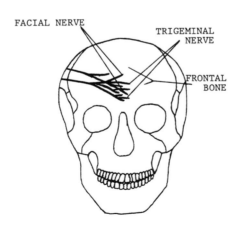

FIGURE 6

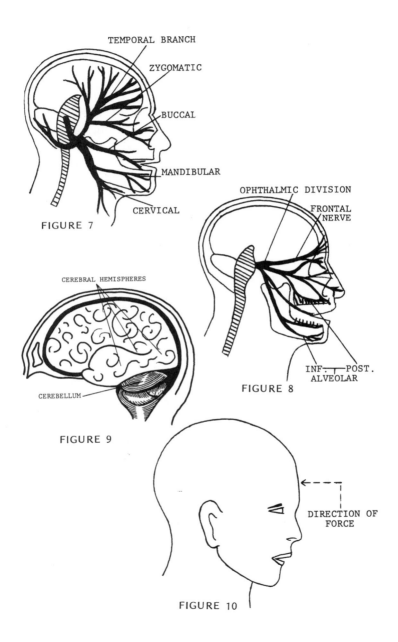

FIGURE 7

TEMPORAL BRANCH

ZYGOMATIC

BUCCAL

MANDIBULAR

CERVICAL

OPHTHALMIC DIVISION

FRONTAL NERVE

INF. POST.
ALVEOLAR

FIGURE 8

CEREBRAL HEMISPHERES

CEREBELLUM

FIGURE 9

DIRECTION OF FORCE

FIGURE 10

Master Long is squared with his opponent in a right lead position again, but this time with the left hand relaxed at the midpoint of the body.

The opponent having advanced with a high section reverse punch, Master Long advances slightly, using a crossing forearm block. Note that the hips, shoulders, and returning strike hand are all cocked.

In his completed movement, the body has completely rotated and locked into position; a reverse punch is thrown to the frontal bone and trigeminal nerve.

Temple and Fossa Temporalis

The temple is actually a recessed bone tip of the sphenoid (figure 11) that surfaces at the temporal region, or more specifically, at the great wings of the sphenoid (figure 12). Figure 13 shows the outer view of the great wings as the tips surface at the sides of the

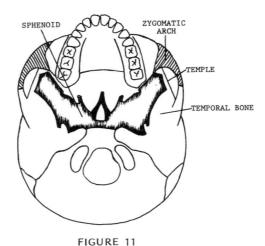

FIGURE 11

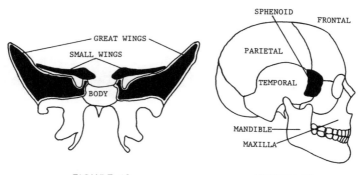

FIGURE 12   FIGURE 13

skull. Referring back to figure 11, note that the zygo-matic arch and temporal bone join to form the fossa temporalis. In summary, the great wings of the sphenoid form the recessed portion of the temple; the zygomatic arch and the temporal bone join to form the fossa tem-poralis at the bottom; and the frontal, parietal, and tem-poral bones form the top and sides of the head.

Additional factors are involved in attacks to the temple. First, there is direct contact to the ophthalmic division of the trigeminal nerve (see figure 8). The tri-geminal nerve controls several facial functions and ex-tends to the main sensory nucleus of the fifth cranial nerve in the pons. Also passing directly through the temple at the exterior tip of the sphenoid lies the

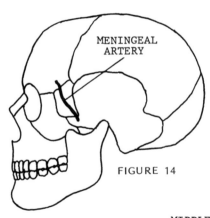

FIGURE 14

MIDDLE MENINGEAL

FIGURE 15

middle meningeal artery, the largest branch supplying the dura matter (figures 14 and 15). Finally, the sphenoid could be jammed directly into the brain with a direct, penetrating blow. With maximum force, the tip of the great wings could break off and enter the brain. The meningeal artery could burst from the impact or be severed by a broken bone or bone chip. Contact to the trigeminal nerve could result in unconsciousness and/or loss of control to several facial functions. Compression of the brain, hemorrhage, concussion, shock, and death are likely results of striking the temple.

The temple should be attacked on a horizontal plane directed toward the opposing temple. This is a class I-D target area.

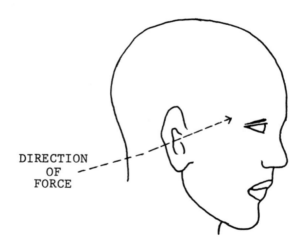

FIGURE 16

Master Long has taken a defensive position in a left lead straddle stance. The right hand is below the elbow, and the body is relaxed.

Opponent's lead is a backhand strike, and Master Long has blocked with a high 90 degree forearm block while stepping back in preparation for his counterstrike.

Master Long has completely rotated his body to power his returning back hand. The left arm remains at the high midsection of the body for defensive purposes.

Eyes

The eyes are beyond a doubt extremely sensitive to even the slightest touch and could easily be poked or pushed from their sockets. The eyes are set deeply into the orbital fissures in the skull (figure 17) and are held in place by the fascia bulbi, a thin membrane between the fatty pads inside the orbital fissure, and by the controlling muscles (figure 18). Approximately five-sixths of the eyeball lies recessed in the orbit, leaving only the small anterior surface exposed. The elasticity of the intrinsic muscles, however, make it easy to poke the eyeball out of the orbital fissure without actually severing the muscles. In striking the eyes, a watering, or secretion of the lacrimal gland, would begin immediately, even with the slightest touch. A blow passing through the anterior chamber into the pupil or lens (fig-

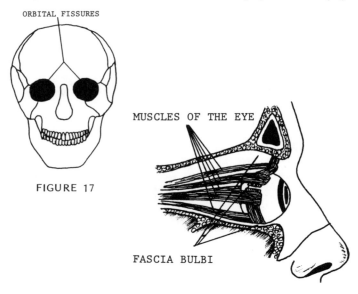

ORBITAL FISSURES

FIGURE 17

MUSCLES OF THE EYE

FASCIA BULBI

FIGURE 18

ure 19) would cause the vitreous body to leak into the posterior and anterior chambers. Needless to say, temporary blindness could occur from any minor penetration of the eye. If a strike did penetrate the posterior cavity into the vitreous body, the eyeball would collapse, almost certainly causing permanent loss of sight to that eye.

The results of striking the eyes could range from minor pain and eye watering to shock, unconsciousness, permanent blindness and/or loss of the afflicted eye. Striking the eye could also be a death blow because, with deep penetration of a finger strike, the brain would be penetrated. Figure 20 shows the preferred direction in which force should be applied for this class II-B target.

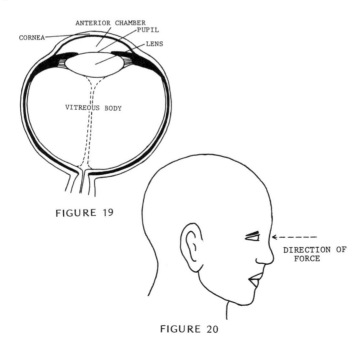

ANTERIOR CHAMBER
PUPIL
CORNEA
LENS

VITREOUS BODY

FIGURE 19

DIRECTION OF
FORCE

FIGURE 20

Master Long and his opponent are squared off in an opposing lead. Opponent is left-faced, Master Long is right-faced.

Advancing with a thrust at the throat, the opponent is blocked with an outer forearm and grapple technique; Master Long has simultaneously prepared his left hand for the return strike.

Retaining his grip on the arm that was blocked, Master Long forces the arm to cross his opponent's body and returns a claw hand thrust to the eyes.

Ears

When properly struck, the ears yield a variety of immobilizing effects, some resulting in permanent damage. Air is easily trapped in the external acoustic meatus and forced down the tube into the tympanic membrane, or eardrum (figure 21). Most commonly, the eardrum will burst, rupturing the malleus, or hammer, the portion known as the middle ear. Damages would cause extreme pain, loss of hearing, bleeding from the mouth and ear, and bleeding into the throat via the internal auditory tube. Figure 22 shows a view of the middle ear from the external acoustic meatus. Note that the first obstruction in the tube is the tympanic membrane, or eardrum. The strategic value of this pres-

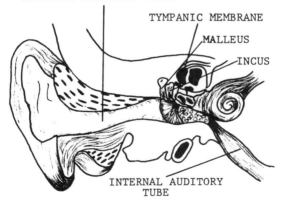

EXTERNAL ACOUSTIC MEATUS

TYMPANIC MEMBRANE

MALLEUS

INCUS

INTERNAL AUDITORY TUBE

FIGURE 21

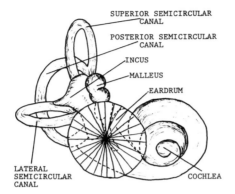

SUPERIOR SEMICIRCULAR CANAL

POSTERIOR SEMICIRCULAR CANAL

INCUS

MALLEUS

EARDRUM

LATERAL SEMICIRCULAR CANAL

COCHLEA

FIGURE 22

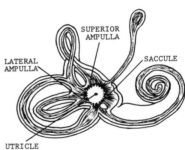

SUPERIOR AMPULLA

LATERAL AMPULLA

SACCULE

UTRICLE

FIGURE 23

sure point exceeds the majority of the forty-three tar-get areas listed in this study in that a high level of pain is rendered, and the malfunction of a sensory organ is achieved. In addition, the nucleus of physical combat is broken *balance!* Behind the middle ear lies the inner ear, the center of equilibrium for the cerebellum (fig-ure 23). The cerebellum (figure 24) links the impulses that arise from stimulation of the sensory nerves of the vestibular apparatus to the motor centers of the cerebrum that maintain posture and equilibrium. Receptors for the vestibular apparatus are located in the utricle of the inner ear. A sufficient force applied to the ear could therefore render an opponent helpless. If unconsciousness did not occur, the opponent would be unable to stand, due to the loss of equilibrium. Permanent damage to the vestibular receptors and tympanic membrane could result.

Figure 25 shows the preferred direction in which force should be applied. The ears are a class II-B target area.

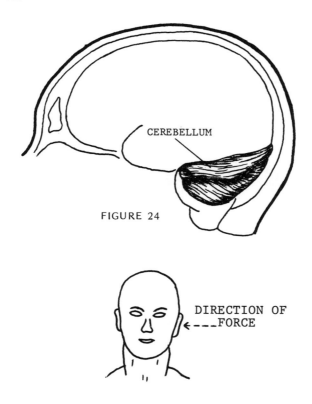

CEREBELLUM

FIGURE 24

DIRECTION OF
←---FORCE

FIGURE 25

Master Long gripped in a double hand chokehold from the front.

In his first maneuver, Master Long tenses his neck muscles and forces his head forward. While doing this he steps back with his left leg and cocks his hands for his next movement.

Having ensured his balance with the forward stance, Master Long now breaks the opponent's grip in an upward thrust, using the muscles of the arms and shoulders, the right thigh muscle, and the muscles of the lower back. Notice that the leaning position shown in the second illustration is now an erect position. The hands have also been cocked for the return attack.

His return attack is a cupped hand strike to the ears. The blow is powered in the same manner as a palm-up suto to the neck or temple area.

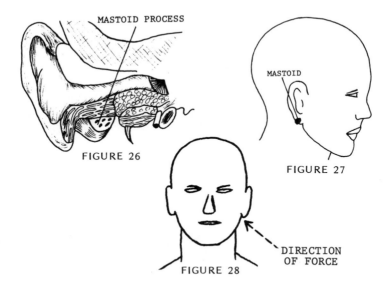

FIGURE 26

FIGURE 27

FIGURE 28

DIRECTION
OF FORCE

Mastoid

The mastoid is the protuberance just behind the ear and is filled with many air pockets communicating directly with the middle ear (figure 26). The mastoid would not be considered a preferred target if it were not for the great pain involved when pressure is applied to the area. Because of its recessed position behind the ear (figure 27), the mastoid should not be attacked with a thrust. In close contact, such as a front bear hug under the arms, applying foreknuckle or thumbnail pressure to the mastoid would make it an effective target. If pressure to the area is prolonged, damage to the auditory system could occur.

Figure 27 shows the location of the mastoid. Note that the mastoid is almost completely hidden by the earlobe. The mastoid is a II-A class target area. Figure 28 shows the preferred direction in which force should be applied.

Master Long is grabbed from the front with a typical lapel or jacket grab.

Master Long begins his defensive maneuver by placing the right hand on his opponent's left mastoid area, and placing the left foreknuckle of the index finger into the right mastoid.

Even as a practice maneuver and with a small amount of pressure, the pain cannot be withstood, and the opponent will instinctively pull away. For street use, pressure should be applied in a squeezing motion retaining the grip on the opposite side of the head, and of course, maximum pressure should be applied.

Septal Cartilage

The septal cartilage is more commonly referred to as the nose. It is the external portion of the respiratory system which partially protrudes from the face (figure 29). The internal portions of the nose are much greater in size and functional necessity than the external portions. The septal cartilage rests in the nasal cavity, located in the central portion of the face (figure 30). Referring back to figure 29, note that the only solid formation behind the nasal bone and septal cartilage is the crista galli, a small, multipocketed bone formation. The internal nasal process and the crista galli are all that stand between the septal cartilage and the brain. A direct horizontal strike to the nose could break the septal cartilage and the nasal bone, rupturing the nasal portion of the angular vein. Profuse bleeding would result, and sinus reactions would occur in the frontals,

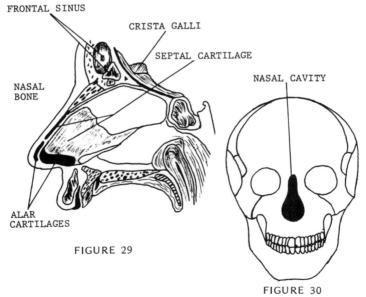

FRONTAL SINUS

CRISTA GALLI

SEPTAL CARTILAGE

NASAL CAVITY

NASAL BONE

ALAR CARTILAGES

FIGURE 29

FIGURE 30

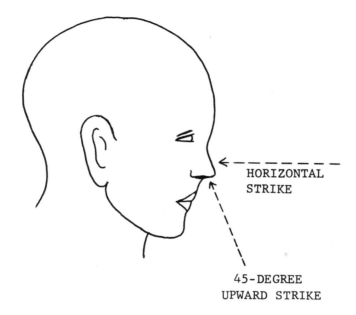

HORIZONTAL
STRIKE

45-DEGREE
UPWARD STRIKE

FIGURE 31

causing tearing of the eyes (figure 29). Though such a blow would inflict great pain, it would not necessarily stop an aggressor. However, striking that same target with an upward movement at a 45-degree angle could easily result in death by forcing the septal cartilage through the internal portions of the nose and through the crista galli into the brain (figure 31). Death would be almost instantaneous, due largely to compression of the brain.

Classifying this target will be done according to the direction of the blow, since strikes made at different angles have such drastically different results. Struck on a horizontal plane, the septal cartilage would be a class II-A target. When struck on a 45-degree upward plane, the septal cartilage would be a II-D target area.

The opponent has taken a shifted cat position, and Master Long has taken a similar stance with his hands located along the life line.

The opponent has attempted a feint and a lower middle gate punch. Master Long shifts to an advanced straddle stance and has used a palm-down block, extending his arm to a cocked position in preparation for his initial return attack.

From the block, Master Long's first counterattack is a horizontal strike, done by rotating the hand in a semicircular movement and striking the nose with the back of the wrist, dislodging the nose from the nasal cavity.

In his final thrust, the hips and shoulders are rotated in the direction of the attacking palm strike at a 45-degree angle. The opponent would die as a result of the septal cartilage penetrating the brain.

Anterior Nasal Spine

The anterior nasal spine, located between the nose and upper lip, is most sensitive closer to the nose, as indicated by the V formation in figure 32. Referring back to figure 8, note that the nerve supply is the anterior alveolar branch of the facial nerve. Because the facial nerve is struck when contacting the anterior nasal spine, the sensory fibers would relay the shock to the pons, causing the dizziness that is characteristic of striking other sensory tips of the facial nerve.

More advantageous than the neurological reaction is the structural damage to the fragile bone tip, the maxilla, and the gums and teeth, which would involve the posterior alveolar, another branch of the facial nerve (figure 8). Extensive bleeding could result from breaking the gums and teeth and would have more effect psychologically than physiologically. Sinus response would cause eye tearing and nasal congestion.

The anterior nasal spine will be a class I-A target area; the preferred direction of force is indicated in figure 33.

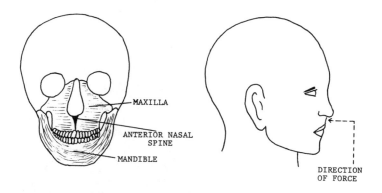

MAXILLA

ANTERIOR NASAL SPINE

MANDIBLE

DIRECTION OF FORCE

FIGURE 32   FIGURE 33

Master Long has assumed a high crane position against his opponent.

Feinting a kick to draw in his opponent, Master Long blocks a high section reverse punch with a palm-up inside forearm block.

In his final movement, Master Long forces the blocked arm across his opponent's body grasping it at the wrist, and returns a reverse punch to the anterior nasal spine. Note that again the hips and shoulders have been rotated.

Temporomandibular Joint

The temporomandibular joint, more commonly known as the jaw hinge, is located directly beneath the temporal bone (zygoma) in front of the ear (figure 34). Angles of attack and use of the mandible are important factors for maximum effectiveness in attacking this area. To begin, the temporomandibular joint can only dislocate in a forward direction. This would most easily occur as the result of a downward 45-degree blow to the chin. When the jaw is fully in the open position, pressure can be felt in the lower extremity of the joint. Since the temporomandibular joint actually consists of two joints, dislocation can be unilateral or bilateral, depending whether one or both joints are displaced (see looped articulation in figure 34). Since the temporomandibular joint moves freely, it is best to first trap the neck movement to one side or the other. There are two points of absorption in the attack. One is of course the temporomandibular joint itself, and the other is the horizontal rotation of the neck. To break the joint with the least amount of force, it is best to strike when the head is completely rotated to one side or the other (figure 35), because the absorption from the neck is

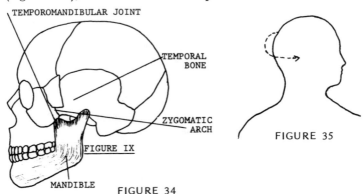

TEMPOROMANDIBULAR JOINT

TEMPORAL BONE

ZYGOMATIC ARCH

FIGURE IX

MANDIBLE   FIGURE 34

FIGURE 35

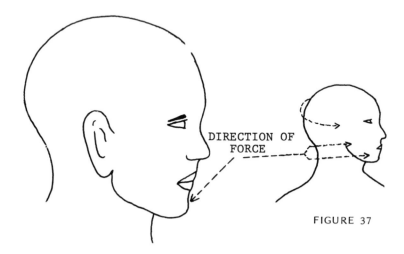

DIRECTION OF
FORCE

FIGURE 37

FIGURE 36

thus minimized. Striking either the joint or the mandible for leverage with the head in this position would
most easily break the articulation with sufficient force.
The nerve supply is from the fifth cranial nerve, being
the auriculotemporal branch. The profuse bleeding inci-
dental to a broken jaw is supplied by the deep auricular
branch of the internal maxillary artery.

The preferred direction of force would depend on
the desired result. Striking the point of the mandible
at a 45-degree downward angle (figure 36) would result
in dislocation. Striking the side of the mandible or the
hinge itself on a horizontal plane (figure 37) would
break the joint. The temporomandibular joint is a class
V-A target area.

Here Master Long's opponent
sets in front of him prepared
to attack.

The opponent attempts a low
reverse punch, and Master
Long has executed a low outer
forearm block while advancing
to set up his counterattack.

Master Long has delivered a vertical punch to his opponent's mandible to lock the neck into place for his next attack.

His final movement is the delivery of a reverse punch at the jaw hinge. With the head rotated, the jaw will absorb full pressure of the blow.

Tip of the Mandible

The tip of the mandible is often referred to as the "button" in boxing circles. Boxing is not particularly scientific in contact points because permissible striking areas are very limited. Unlike strikes used in martial arts studies where anatomical weapons are developed and focused into the smallest possible areas, the contact point of a boxing glove is distributed over its large cushioned surface. But even with a glove, striking the tip of the mandible means a quick K.O. when struck at the proper angle. Figures 38 and 39 point out the precise location.

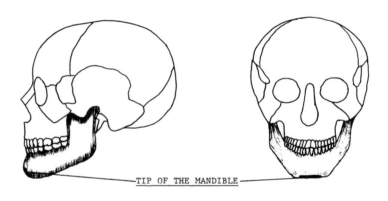

TIP OF THE MANDIBLE

FIGURE 38   FIGURE 39

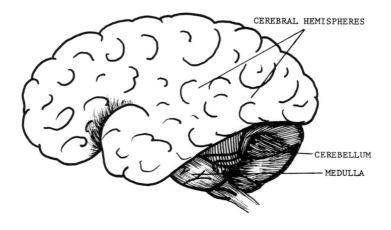

FIGURE 40

To begin, let us first examine not the action, but the *re-action* of the blow, and that reaction is to the medulla and the cerebellum. Figures 40 and 41 show the location of the critical brain areas and the transfer of shock causing the reactions from these areas.

Shock to the cerebellum and to the cerebral hemispheres, as previously discussed in pressure point 2, will cause unconsciousness. The chart in figure 42 illustrates how the shock transfer to the medulla is equally an attack to the autonomic nervous system, involving the heart and lungs. Sufficient jarring force will cause split-second arrest to the heart and lungs. The result would of course be unconsciousness. A final factor involved is the

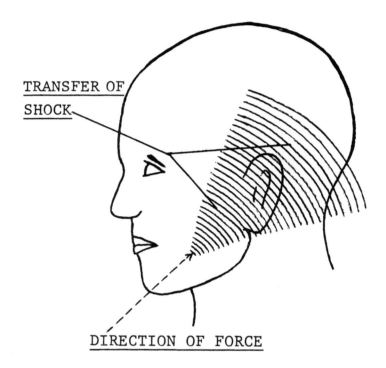

TRANSFER OF
SHOCK

DIRECTION OF FORCE

FIGURE 41

contact to the trigeminal nerve (see figure 7, mandibular). Contact to the trigeminal nerve could result in
unconsciousness, as discussed in pressure point 2. Because of the many factors involved and the positive
striking results, the tip of the mandible is a preferred
target area. This is a class I-C target area.

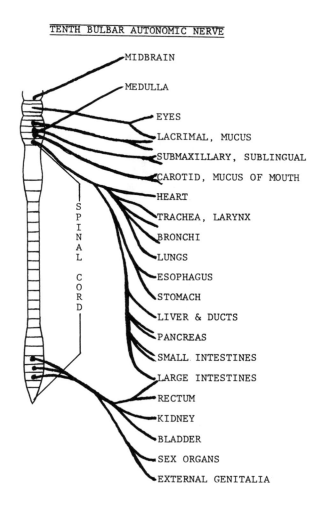

FIGURE 42

Master Long has assumed a cat position as his opponent begins an overhand lunge at his head.

With Master Long's hand raised high, the opponent decides to change his attack and try an uppercut to the solar plexus.

Seeing the change of direction in time, Master Long changes his block and slams a hard forearm block into his attacker's arm.

Having advanced with the block, Master Long easily reaches his opponent's chin, delivering a rising 45-degree upward knockout punch.

Sternocleidomastoid Region

The sternocleidomastoid region describes the area at the frontal sides of the neck. There is much more here than meets the eye. The muscle itself represents only a third of the three-point target area's sensitivities. Lying directly under this muscle are the carotid artery and the jugular vein. Both cross at a common area directly under the sternocleidomastoid muscle, as illustrated in figure 44.

Beginning with the sternocleidomastoid (figure 45), the muscle originates at the upper sternum and lower inner border of the clavicle, and inserts at the lateral surface of the mastoid process. Functionally, one side flexes the cervical vertebral column laterally and rotates it. Both muscles acting together flex the cervical system, moving the head toward the back and thus elevating the chin. As for sensitivity, test it yourself. Poke the area lightly with your forefinger. As you increase the poking pressure, you will feel a jar at the opposite side of the head. The pain, according to how hard you dare strike

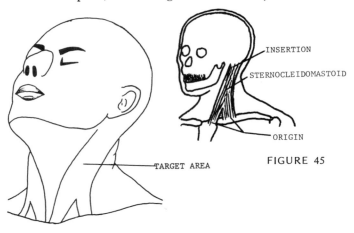

INSERTION

STERNOCLEIDOMASTOID

ORIGIN

TARGET AREA

FIGURE 45

FIGURE 43

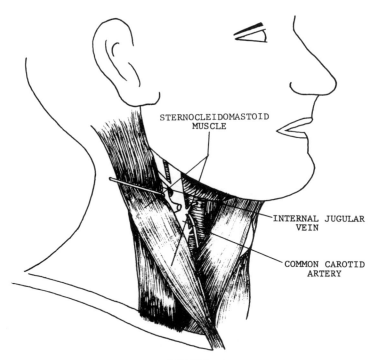

STERNOCLEIDOMASTOID
MUSCLE

INTERNAL JUGULAR
VEIN

COMMON CAROTID
ARTERY

FIGURE 44

yourself, will be felt on both sides of the muscle and
inner and outer surfaces. Contraction and dizziness
would be the intitial responses to a strike of medium
force. Referring back to figure 44, the more serious
physiological responses would come from the carotid
artery and the jugular vein. A blow of sufficient force
could blister, swell, collapse, or burst one or both of the
major blood lines whose most important function is supplying the blood transactions of the brain. Figure 46
shows the neck area from a front view and the track
lines of the jugular vein and carotid artery as they lie in
the neck. The jugular vein functions as the return line to
the heart from the brain, and the carotid artery feeds

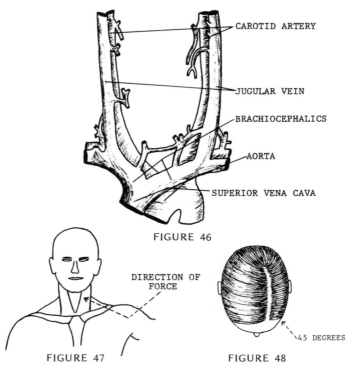

CAROTID ARTERY

JUGULAR VEIN

BRACHIOCEPHALICS

AORTA

SUPERIOR VENA CAVA

FIGURE 46

DIRECTION OF
FORCE

45 DEGREES

FIGURE 47   FIGURE 48

blood to the brain from the heart. Interrupting the
blood flow to or from the brain could easily have fatal
consequences. In cardiopulmonary resuscitation, a high
emphasis is placed on pumping the heart more times per
cycle than breathing air into victims of shock, cardiac
arrest, and drowning because without blood, the brain
will immediately begin to deteriorate. Any interruption
of the blood flow will immediately cause dizziness, unconsciousness, and possible death.

Striking the sternocleidomastoid region should be
done on an upsloping plane at 45 degrees as illustrated
in figures 47 and 48. Pressure point 11 is a class III-D
target area.

Assuming a low cross stance, Master Long prepares to deflect his opponent's attack.

Attempting a low reverse punch, the opponent's blow is deflected at the wrist and grappled as Master Long prepares his counterattack.

The completed move leaves Master Long's heel thrust deeply into his opponent's sternocleidomastoid region.

Anterior Neck Region

The anterior neck region is the surgical area at the frontal center portion of the neck, more commonly referred to as the *windpipe* or *throat.* A strike to this area can be lethal for several reasons. As we examine the area, a more realistic view will come into focus on the seriousness of an attack to the anterior neck region.

The esophagus is a collapsible tube about ten inches long through which food enters the digestive system. It extends from the pharynx to the stomach, piercing the diaphragm in its descent from the thorax to the abdominal cavity, behind the trachea and the heart (figure 49). The larynx, also shown in figure 49, is the communicating opening between the trachea and the esophagus, and controls the integration and segregation of air or matter that passes through their tubes. The thyroid cartilage,

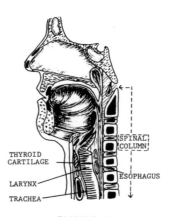

FIGURE 50

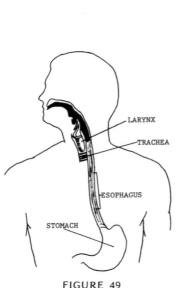

FIGURE 49

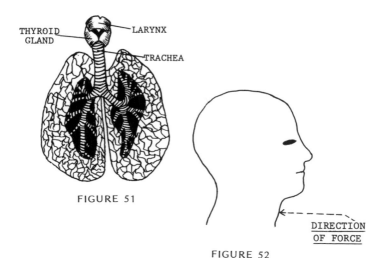

THYROID GLAND — LARYNX

—TRACHEA

FIGURE 51

DIRECTION
OF FORCE

FIGURE 52

or Adam's apple, assists the larynx in that function (figure 50). The trachea is the air tube leading to the lungs (figure 51). It is located in front of the esophagus and is lined with C-shaped rings made of hyaline cartilage. When the anterior neck region is struck, the thyroid and hyaline cartilages may be broken or otherwise forced through the larynx and/or the trachea, resulting in blood drowning or partial or complete obstruction of the vital air passages.

Because of their vital functions, the internal portions of the anterior neck region are a critical target. Virtually exposed to the slightest pressure, they are protected by only a layer of skin. The hyaline cartilages that hold the trachea in a cylindrical shape will serve as puncturing or cutting devices only when properly stuck. Any swelling in the area will cut short or completely constrict the windpipe, possibly resulting in asphyxiation. Blood drowning is likely where sufficient force is applied. Figure 52 shows the proper angle of attack.

Master Long has taken a shift horse stance against his opponent's modified cat position.

Attacked with a side lunge punch, Master Long has blocked with an open palm block and leaned away to begin the spinning motion for his next maneuver.

In his final move, Master Long has countered with a spinning heel kick. The art of this strike has been lost in most of today's martial arts. Note that the heel is placed in the focus point to effect maximum kill power. The flat bottom of the foot is also effective, but the heel should be used to exert the greatest possible force.

Brachial Plexus and Trapezius Muscle

An opponent's trapezius muscle can be struck from the front or rear because of its protrusion at the shoulders (figures 53 and 54). Innervation by the cervicals includes the brachial plexus, which is most readily struck in the darkened area of figure 53. The brachial plexus is part of a nerve complex which supplies the sacral region, and down through the shoulder and arm as far as the wrist. The brachial plexus is a nerve complex of the somatic system connected to the fifth, sixth, and seventh cervical vertebrae and the first thoracic

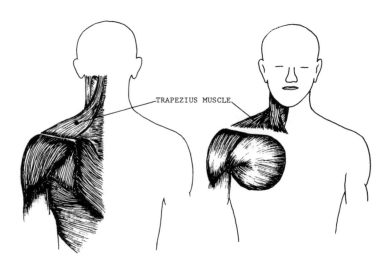

TRAPEZIUS MUSCLE

FIGURE 53   FIGURE 54

vertebrae (figure 55). Because this plexus reaches to the ends of the arms, temporary paralysis could occur on a local level: striking the plexus on the right side could paralyze the right shoulder and arm. Figure 55 shows the origin of the brachial plexus at the cervical vertebrae. Unconsciousness and temporary local paralysis is prevalent with maximum force blows, and permanent paralysis can result.

Figures 56 and 57 show the direction in which force should be applied to this IV-C class target area.

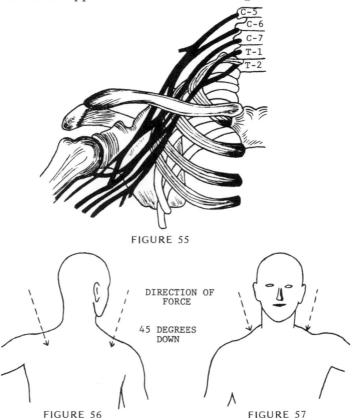

C-5
C-6
C-7
T-1
T-2

FIGURE 55

DIRECTION OF
FORCE

45 DEGREES
DOWN

FIGURE 56   FIGURE 57

Master Long is grabbed around the throat from the front.

The grabbing hand has been struck at the radial nerve with a suto, and Master Long has positioned himself for a counterattack.

In his third and final maneuver, Master Long rotates his hips, shoulders, and stance into the direction of his counterstrike to the brachial plexus.

Suprasternal Notch

The suprasternal notch is a regional description of the area sometimes referred to as the *chicken breast* (figure 58). Note that both collarbones meet and join here. A surface blow could dislodge both collarbones from the sternum, collapsing the shoulders. Although this would be devastating, more crucial targets lie behind the area (figure 59). The aorta and the superior vena cava supply blood to and from the major tracts to the brain (figure 48). The trachea passes behind the aorta and the superior vena cava at the area marked by three *X*'s in figure 58 (see also figures 46 and 48). Because of the cartilaginous framework of the trachea (figures 49 and 50), a blow here could puncture one or more of the major blood tracts. Even without cartilaginous puncture, a forceful strike could still burst, puncture, or otherwise damage these vital blood lines. Without extensive detail on physiological responses,

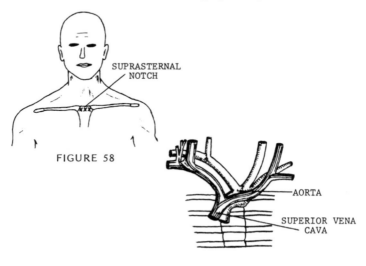

FIGURE 58

FIGURE 59

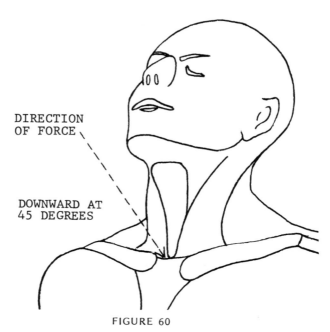

DIRECTION
OF FORCE

DOWNWARD AT
45 DEGREES

FIGURE 60

attacks to this area could indeed be critical, and prob-
ably fatal. Initially, shock and unconsciousness would
occur. The most probable result from a forceful blow to
the suprasternal notch would follow a series of reactions. The strike would dislodge both clavicles from the
sternum; the sternum would split; the two clavicles and
the sternum would be forced against, or puncture, the
aorta and superior vena cava; the cartilages and bones
would then be forced against, or puncture, the trachea;
the hyaline cartilages would be cracked, broken, or
forced through the trachea into the esophagus, and
could easily puncture the aorta and superior vena cava.
It should be obvious by now that the suprasternal
notch is a death target. Figure 60 shows the preferred
direction in which force should be applied. This pressure
point is a class III-D target area.

Master Long and his opponent are squared off in opposing lead positions; both stances are close and poised for quick movement.

Opponent advances with a vertical lunge punch, and Master Long has stepped outside. Only widening his stance and not yet shifting, he simultaneously blocks with the outer forearm and grapple while delivering a thrusting wrist strike to the chin area, thus elevating the head and exposing his next target.

In his third and final movement, Master Long rotates the hips, legs, and shoulders, powering an overhand hammer strike centered at the suprasternal notch.

Clavicle

The clavicle, more commonly known as the collar-bone, is a long bone with a double curvature (figure 61), placed horizontally at the upper anterior portion of the thorax above the first rib (figure 62). The inner end articulates with the sternum and is called the sternal extremity. The outer or aromial end articulates with the scapula.

Figure 63 shows a close-up view of the articulation of the clavicle and the acromion process portion of the scapula. The skeletal function of the clavicles is to give

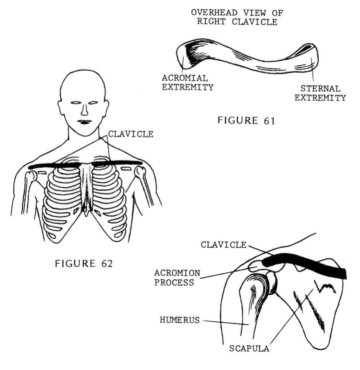

OVERHEAD VIEW OF
RIGHT CLAVICLE

ACROMIAL
EXTREMITY

STERNAL
EXTREMITY

FIGURE 61

CLAVICLE

FIGURE 62

CLAVICLE

ACROMION
PROCESS

HUMERUS

SCAPULA

FIGURE 63

support to the shoulders and the thorax. Breaking a clavicle would collapse the shoulder on the same side. Additional complications would occur if the broken bone were to puncture a lung or the vital body portions discussed in pressure point 14. A simple break with no other complications would of course immobilize the attacker, due to the structural damage and pain. Figure 64 shows the proper angle of attack. The clavicle is a class V-B target area.

DIRECTION OF FORCE:

45 DEGREES INWARD
AND DOWN

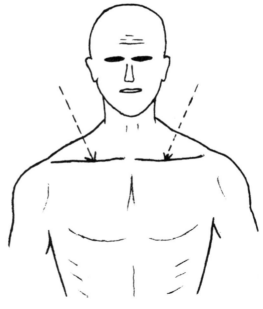

FIGURE 64

Master Long is grabbed by the shoulder from the side.

In his first move, Master Long has begun a wrap movement and cocked his left hand in preparation for a counter-attack.

In his final maneuver, Master Long has completed the arm wrap. The hand of the opponent is locked under his arm, and the elbow is being held firmly by the right hand. Having simultaneously rotated his hips, shoulders, and stance, Master Long delivers an overhand suto strike to the collarbone.

2. Dragons Strike to the Back

The medial dorsal plane is composed of the back of the torso from the base of the cranium to the waistline, including the backs of the upper limbs. There are nine pressure points in this chapter.

16. Base of the cranium
17. Brachial plexus and trapezius muscle
18. Cervical vertebrae
19. Thoracic vertebrae
20. Ribs
21. Spleen
22. Kidneys
23. Shoulder joint
24. Elbow joints

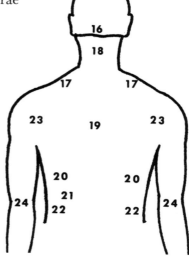

Base of the Cranium

The base of the cranium is located at the rear base of the skull (figure 65) and houses the cerebellum. The trapezius and sternocleidomastoid muscles attach at each side of the target area, leaving only the splenius capitis and cervix muscles to protect the area. Both are sheetlike muscles (figure 66). The deep, smaller muscles in this area would be insignificant to the blow. Referring to figure 67, there are three marked areas at the cranial base: A, B, and C. A and C are the areas that provide the most penetration for jarring the cerebral hemispheres and the pons. B is the area that, when hit, would be most likely to result in a broken neck. A broken neck is, of course, critical and would quickly stop any attacker. It would cause excruciating pain and unconsciousness. However, *where* the neck is broken is of exceeding importance with respect to the physiological response. The odd-shaped vertebra at the base of the skull is num-

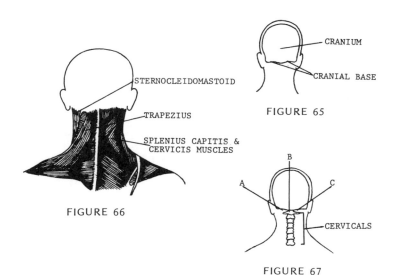

STERNOCLEIDOMASTOID

TRAPEZIUS

SPLENIUS CAPITIS &
CERVICIS MUSCLES

FIGURE 66

CRANIUM

CRANIAL BASE

FIGURE 65

B

A

C

CERVICALS

FIGURE 67

ber one, and the lower vertebrae are numbered progressively; the first seven are cervical. Nerve impulses from the brain feed the nervous system throughout the body via the spinal cord. A basic outline can be found in figure 42. The brachial plexus is made up of the fifth through the eighth cranial nerves and the first thoracic nerve. These nerves are numbered according to their points of origin in the brain. The phrenic nerves and fibers controlling the diaphragm originate between the fifth and sixth cranial nerves before the brachial plexus is formed. An outline of the brachial plexus can be found in figure 55. If the neck is broken, severing or crushing the cervicals above that level, nerve impulses from the brain could not reach the phrenic nerves, and so the diaphragm would cease to contract. The result would be respiratory paralysis, and without artificial respiration the victim would die.

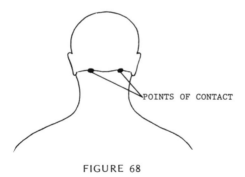

POINTS OF CONTACT

FIGURE 68

ANGLE OF FORCE

FIGURE 69

In conclusion, the base of the cranium must be clas-
sifed according to the angle of attack and the precise
point of contact. Figures 68 and 69 show the proper
angle for force application and the precise area of contact. At this angle and contact point, the base of the
cranium is a class III-C target area. Figures 68 and 69
illustrate the contact points and proper angles for a
knockout result. In figures 70 and 71, the proper
angles and target points for effecting a broken cervical
column above the fifth vertebra are shown. When
attacked according to these illustrations, this pressure
point is classified a V-D target area.

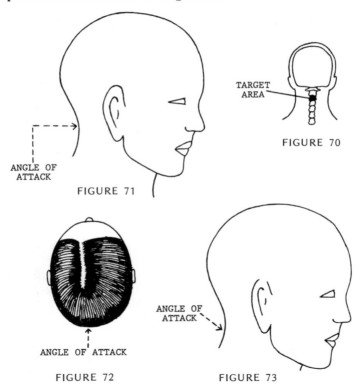

TARGET
AREA

FIGURE 70

ANGLE OF
ATTACK

FIGURE 71

ANGLE OF ATTACK

FIGURE 72

ANGLE OF
ATTACK

FIGURE 73

Master Long has been grabbed by the neck from the front. In beginning his counter, he has placed the right hand on the back of his opponent's neck and thrust a vertical punch into his solar plexus.

The opponent, weakened from the solar plexus strike, is forced down to a 90-degree angle by Master Long's right hand, and Master Long cocks his left hand for his final maneuver.

The completed technique illustrates Master Long delivering an overhand suto strike to the base of the cerebellum. Note the hip and shoulder rotation into the strike as well as the shift of the stance.

Brachial Plexus and Trapezius Muscle

Referring back to pressure point 13, this precious target may be struck from either the frontal plane or the rear, but is more readily struck from the rear. It is again mentioned here for its value in a combat situation, and because of the feasibility of contacting the target with such high-impact blows as the overhead sudo and overhead hammer.

It should again be stressed that the brachial plexus is a potential knockout area, and sufficient force could cause temporary and/or permanent paralysis to the corresponding shoulder and arm. Figure 74 illustrates the location of the trapezius muscle; the brachial plexus is indicated by a dot. Figure 75 shows the direction in which force should be applied. This is a class IV-C target area.

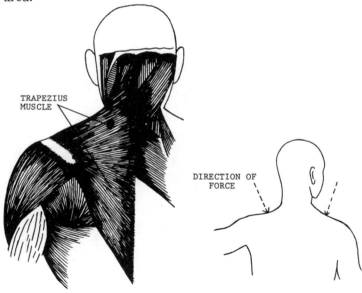

TRAPEZIUS MUSCLE

DIRECTION OF FORCE

FIGURE 74   FIGURE 75

Master Long has been attacked with an advancing side kick and has executed a low block following through and forcing the kick forward, resulting in the advance of his opponent.

His opponent, having regained his balance, is now in an opposing position to Master Long, who has cocked an elbow striking technique.

In his last movement, Master Long has executed a semicircular vertical elbow strike to his opponent's brachial plexus.

Cervical Vertebrae

The cervical vertebrae, as discussed in pressure point 16, are the first top seven vertebrae of the spinal column (figure 76). They are most readily struck at the center-most point of the neck from behind. Structurally, the cervical vertebrae support the neck and head; they also provide a path at their core for the transfer of nerve impulses from the brain throughout the body. The majority of the spinal column pushes against the skin and would thus be an effective target area. The cervicals begin at the base of the cranium and travel the entire length of the neck. It is in this area that the brachial plexus is formed (pressure point 13, figure 55), beginning at the fifth cervical and ending at the first thoracic (figure 76). In pressure point 16 it was stressed that the precise location of the break in the spinal column will determine the result of the attack. Figure 77 is a schematic of the vertebrae showing their location by numbers and how they are anatomically situated. Figure 78 is basically the same illustration, but the vertebrae are exaggerated to display the A and B groups. Numbers one through four make up group A; five through seven

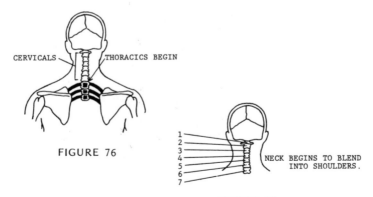

CERVICALS   THORACICS BEGIN

FIGURE 76

NECK BEGINS TO BLEND INTO SHOULDERS.

FIGURE 77

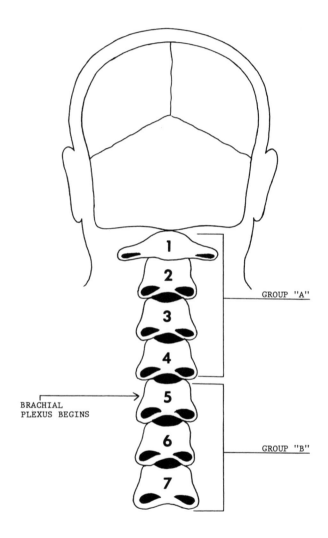

FIGURE 78

make up group B. Severing or pinching the vertebrae in group A would disconnect the phrenic nerves controlling the diaphragm from their origin in the brain. Without innervation, the diaphragm would cease to function, resulting in respiratory paralysis, and causing death. Pinching or severing the vertebrae in group B may have any number of paralyzing effects, but would not cause immediate death, because of the intertwining composition of the brachial plexus. The attack would still of course be extremely serious and would drop any attacker to the ground from shock, pain, and unconsciousness. Preferred striking angles are horizontal or a downward 45-degree angle.

An attack on group A would be a class V-D target. An attack on group B would be a class III-C target.

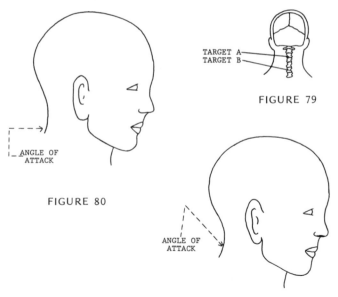

TARGET A
TARGET B

FIGURE 79

ANGLE OF ATTACK

FIGURE 80

ANGLE OF ATTACK

FIGURE 81

Dragons Strike to the Back

Master Long has taken a left lead straddle stance against his opponent.

His opponent having attempted a right backhand strike, Master Long has executed a horizontal palm block and stepped through with his right foot, setting up his return attack.

In his final movement, Master Long has completed a 180-degree turn and delivered a horizontal suto strike to his opponent's cervicals.

Thoracic Vertebrae

The thoracic vertebrae, as depicted in figure 82, are the eighth through the nineteenth vertebrae, a total of twelve vertebrae. They are located at the centermost portion of the back, forming the base of the rib cage. There are twelve pairs of ribs, each pair joined by a thoracic vertebra. The vertebral column is often referred to as the backbone, and the term well describes its function. The vertebrae do, in fact, hold the body erect. In addition to its thoracic and supportive functions, the vertebral column also furnishes a path for nerves to and from the brain, innervating the entire body. The first five thoracics play a major part in the formation of the cardiac plexus (figure 83), a nerve system that assists the

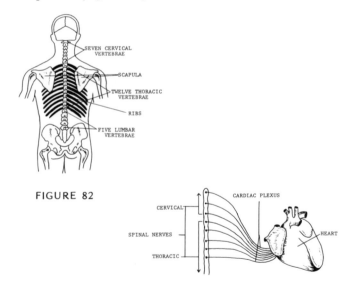

FIGURE 82

FIGURE 83

rhythmic function of the heart. Figure 84 shows a side cutaway view of the vertebrae. The spinal cord actually exists independently, lying in the hollowed-out area of the vertebrae and suspended in a substance called the cerebrospinal fluid. It is through the thoracic vertebrae that the many nerves travel from the medulla. As a target area, the thoracic vertebrae would be hard to miss because of their centered position in the back and because of the length of this spinal segment. An attack to the first five thoracics would be most effective, due to the extra support given to the area by the rib cage and the clavicle. Where more support is given to a target, the target is less likely to give with applied force. The first

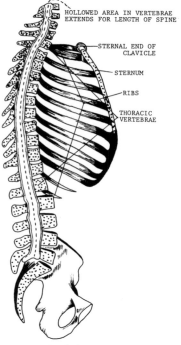

FIGURE 84

five thoracics are also most effective as targets because of the direct contact to the main innervation of the cardiac plexus. Attacking the thoracic vertebrae could result in nervous shock and unconsciousness because of the direct lead into the medulla. When excessive force is used, cardiac arrest may result from nervous relay of the cardiac plexus. Additional complications could arise from the dislodging of one or more ribs or structural damage to the spinal column. Figure 85 illustrates target areas A and B. An attack to A, comprising the first five thoracics, would most readily cause cardiac response. An attack to B would cause any of the named physiological reactions, excluding the cardiac response. Figure 86 shows the angle at which force should be applied. Both 1 and 2 can be applied to the A target area, but only 2 should be applied to target area B. Target area A is a class III-B target; target area B is a V-C target area.

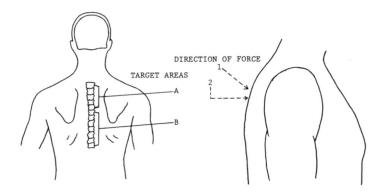

FIGURE 85   FIGURE 86

Master Long has taken a high cat position against his opponent's straddle stance.

The opponent having lunged forward with a backhand strike, Master Long executes a high scoop block, simultaneously cocking his right leg for his return attack.

In the completed movement, Master Long has rotated down the palm of the blocking hand and grappled his opponent's arm while returning the attack with a hook kick to the B group thoracics. Note that the heel is focused on the target.

Ribs

There are a total of twenty-four ribs in the body, twelve pairs joined by the vertebral column at the rear, and by the costal cartilages and sternum in front. There are twelve ribs on each side of the thorax, connected with a thoracic vertebra by the head and tubercle of the posterior extremity. The head fits into a facet formed by the adjacent bodies of two vertebrae. The tubercle articulates with the transverse process (figure 87). Strong ligaments surround and bind these articulations, but permit slight gliding movements.

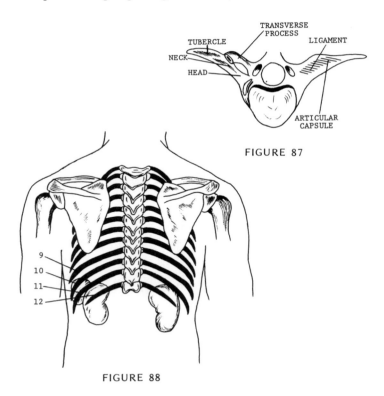

FIGURE 87

FIGURE 88

The left side of figure 87 shows the articulation with the ligaments removed. Figure 88 shows a transparent view of the back to illustrate the joining of the ribs to the thoracic vertebrae. Since the scapula covers most of the ribs from behind (figure 88), the ninth through the twelfth ribs are of most concern. The ninth and tenth ribs wrap around to the front of the body and join the costal cartilage. The eleventh and twelfth do not and are therefore referred to as the floating ribs. Because there is little support to these ribs, it would require more penetration to break them, but the consequences could be more deadly. If the rib is broken, the anterior portion that is severed will float freely inside the body and could easily puncture a vital organ or tract. If the ninth or tenth rib is broken, the ends are still basically held in place. A break in the ninth or tenth rib can prove fatal, but the probability of lethal consequences is greater when the eleventh or twelfth rib is broken.

Figure 89 shows the areas in which the ribs should be attacked for maximum effectiveness, A with respect to the eleventh and twelfth, B with respect to the remaining exposed areas. Figure 90 shows the angles at which force may be applied. The ribs are a class V-B target area.

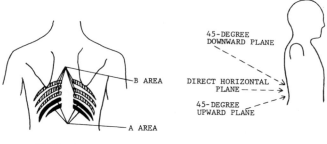

FIGURE 89   FIGURE 90

Here Master Long is in a high cat position, prepared for his opponent's attack.

The opponent attempts an advancing side kick, which Master Long blocks with a 45-degree palm block.

Stepping forward and shifting the hips, shoulders, and stance into the direction of the blow, Master Long delivers a vertical punch to the ribs at the back.

Spleen

The spleen is located directly below the diaphragm above the left kidney and behind the fundus of the stomach. An illustration of the spleen (figure 91) displays its oval shape and venous and arterial tracts. When viewed transparently from the front, the spleen can be seen at the left side through the ribs. Figure 92 illustrates the location. As a target area, the spleen is most accessible from the left rear side of the torso, as shown in figure 93.

The spleen serves as a blood reservoir because of its many venous spaces, but its basic function is the destruction of red blood cells and platelets. Even though it is considered a major tract organ, it can be bypassed and removed by surgery without serious consequences. While in the body, however, the spleen may be effectively attacked with resultant blood-flow interference trauma and hemorrhage. The spleen would be considerably increased in size while the body was fighting an

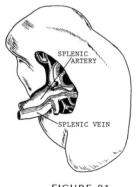

FIGURE 91

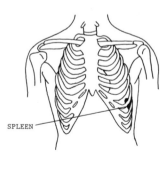

FIGURE 92

infectious disease and would therefore be prone to
cause greater pain if attacked at that time. Normally the
blood volume of the spleen is about 350 ml. If hemorrhage occurred somewhere in the body, the sympathetic
nervous system would stimulate the spleen to increase
blood flow, reducing the reservoir to 200 ml in less than
a minute, functioning as a sort of self-transfusion. A
blow to the spleen is very painful, but requires a deep
penetrating force. The blow could cause hemorrhage,
pain, and trauma. Full-force contact could cause internal damage requiring surgical removal of the organ. Figure 94 illustrates the target area; figure 95 shows the
angle of attack for this III-A class target area.

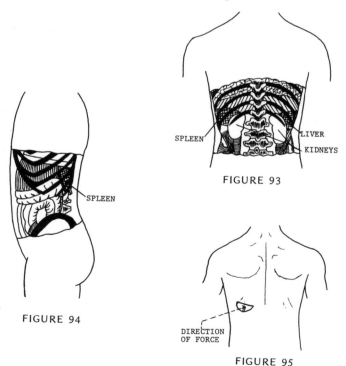

FIGURE 93

FIGURE 94

FIGURE 95

Here Master Long assumes a shifted cat position against his opponent's shifted back stance.

A short advance lunge punch is blocked and pushed far away, rotating the opponent's body to expose his spleen to attack.

A vertical right punch is delivered to the spleen. Note again that Master Long's hips, shoulders, and stance have been rotated in the direction of the attack.

Kidneys

Nutrients added to the bloodstream by the digestive organs and oxygen from the lungs are utilized by cells of the body for growth and repair, for synthesis of hormones or other secretions, and as a source of energy for these and other cell activities. As a result of the complex chemical reactions taking place within the cell, certain products are formed that tend to alter the normal internal and external environment of the cell. Unless these conditions are kept in their normal range, cell functioning will begin to deteriorate, resulting in death of the cell, and possibly of the person. The kidneys are the organs most responsible for maintaining homeostasis of the body fluids. The kidneys are the heart of the urinary system (figure 96) and are termed *excretory glands*. The kidneys function to eliminate metabolic end products of protein, urea, uric acid, creatine, and water. To summarize their primary function, which is important to understand, the kidneys create, collect, and excrete

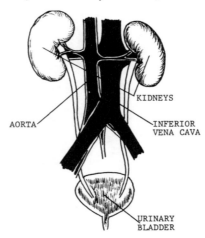

FIGURE 96

urine. When the kidneys do not function properly, the body is poisoned internally. Innervation is derived from the renal plexus, which is formed from branches of the celiac and aortic plexuses, and the splanchnic nerves. The blood supply is furnished by the renal artery, which is a branch of the abdominal aorta.

The kidneys are located just under and extending down from the twelfth rib, on either side of the spinal column. The kidneys resemble lima beans in shape. An average-sized kidney measures approximately four and one-half inches in length, two to three inches in width, and one inch in thickness. Usually the left kidney is slightly larger than the right. The liver pushes the right kidney down to a level somewhat lower than the left. A heavy cushion of fat normally keeps the kidneys up in position. Connective tissue anchors the kidneys to surrounding structures and also helps to maintain their normal position.

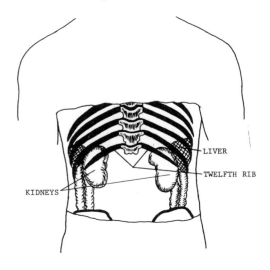

FIGURE 97

Striking a kidney would be comparable to squeezing a balloon filled with water; a stretching or bursting would occur. The many pockets of blood could burst or tear as a result of the strike, due to compression. The pain involved is excruciating and long-lived. A hard blow to the kidneys is often followed by several days of soreness and blood in the urine. Permanent damage forcing the removal of the organ could occur.

The precise area is illustrated in figure 98. Figures 99 and 100 show the proper angles at which force should be applied. The kidneys are a class III-B or III-A target area.

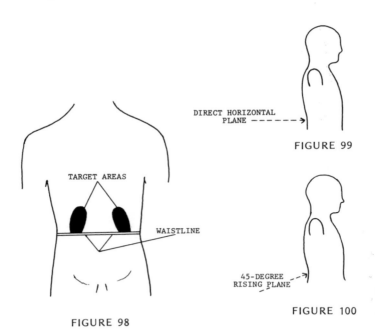

FIGURE 98

FIGURE 99

FIGURE 100

Both combatants are in a right-faced position. Master Long has assumed a cat form; his opponent is in a shifted straddle.

Following a feint, his opponent attempts a backhand strike to the head. Master Long has blocked the hand with an almost-extended palm block and brought up his left leg in readiness for his follow-up maneuver.

In his final movement, Master Long delivers a bridge kick to his opponent's kidney. This picture does not illustrate the completion of the movement, which would leave both legs locked at the knee.

HOW MANY DO YOU REMEMBER SO FAR?

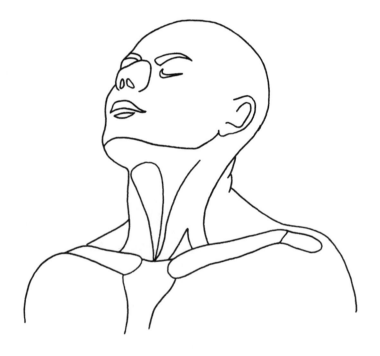

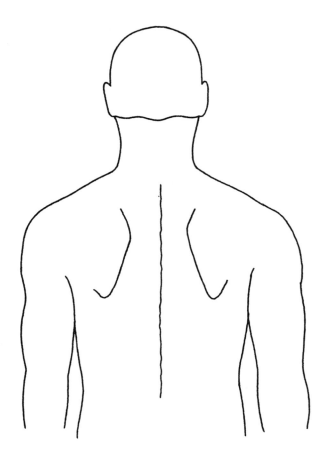

Shoulder Joint

The shoulder joint is a ball-and-socket joint allowing free movement between the scapula and the humerus (figures 101 and 102). Figure 101 is the front view of the joint (A), and figure 102 is the rear view of the joint (B). Note that in the A view, the clavicle holds the scapulae in their spanned position across the shoulders. In the B view, note that the scapula rests outside the rib cage in the back. The shoulder girdle has functions that do not include the use of the humerus, such as shrugging or the rear flexing of the shoulders. These and other movements of the shoulder are of no value with reference to pressure point targets. The movement of concern is that between the scapula and the humerus. The shoulder joint can be positioned for dislocation with a strike, or the radius and humerus can be locked and used as a leverage point to dislocate the shoulder.

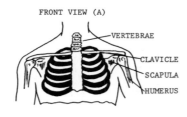

FRONT VIEW (A)

VERTEBRAE

CLAVICLE

SCAPULA

HUMERUS

FIGURE 101

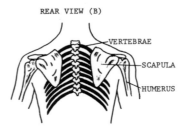

REAR VIEW (B)

VERTEBRAE

SCAPULA

HUMERUS

FIGURE 102

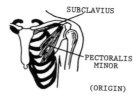

FIGURE 103

FIGURE 106

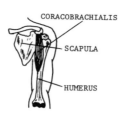

FIGURE 104

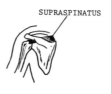

FIGURE 107

FIGURE 105

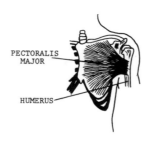

FIGURE 108

Sprain may be accomplished with the same techniques using-less force. In the following series of drawings, a close-up view of the joint is shown, and the muscle and cartilage insertions illustrate the strenghtening of the joint. Figure 103 is the only illustration not directly involved with the humerus motion. To determine what motion is accomplished in the remaining figures, look at the origin and insertion points of the muscles. Every muscle in the human torso pulls; no muscle pushes. With that in mind, it is easy to figure out how each muscle moves the humerus.

It would be impossible to graphically illustrate the assorted techniques used to apply pressure to the shoulder joint. For the purpose of this book, the illustration below displays basic pressure angles. With the arm extended and the palm turned up, the joint is in its maximum open position, and it is most likely to dislocate in that position. Pressure point 23 is a class V-A target area.

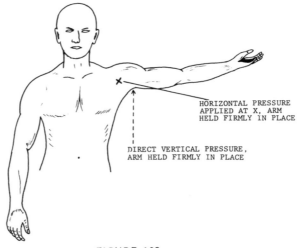

FIGURE 109

The opponent has drawn a club on Master Long.

Meeting his swing, Master Long shifts into a forward stance and lifts an inside suto block high, which will cause the opponent's arm to slide along the outside of his body. At the same time, Master Long cocks his left arm for his return strike.

In his final movement, Master Long has wrapped and locked the arm, and delivers a 45-degree hammer strike to the front of the shoulder joint.

Elbow Joints

The elbow joint, like the shoulder joint, is not a pressure point per se. It is a sensitive area when proper technique is applied, but is also an extremely powerful weapon when flexed. To utilize the elbow joint as a target area, proper positioning is required. Figures 110 through 113 show the elbow joints in different postures, viewed in the opened or locked position. When in a locked position, the elbow can readily be used as a pressure point, with serious consequence to the victim. As the illustrations clearly depict, the elbow joint binds two bones to one. A break in the articulations, depending on where the break is made, could result in the surgical removal of the joint and replacement with a mechanical hinge. A blow to the elbow with properly applied force and angle is extremely painful, even if the joint is not severed.

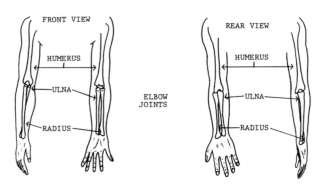

FIGURE 110   FIGURE 111

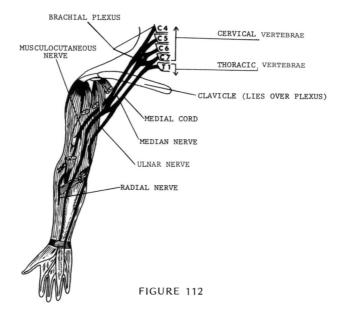

BRACHIAL PLEXUS

MUSCULOCUTANEOUS
NERVE

C4
C5
C6
C7
T1

CERVICAL VERTEBRAE

THORACIC VERTEBRAE

CLAVICLE (LIES OVER PLEXUS)

MEDIAL CORD

MEDIAN NERVE

ULNAR NERVE

RADIAL NERVE

FIGURE 112

Innervation is from the median and ulnar nerves
originating from the brachial plexus, which account for
the pain reception in the area (figure 112). The ulnar
nerve, one of the most frequently contacted nerves in
the body, is located in this branch. Often referred to as
the funny bone, the ulnar nerve, as illustrated, feeds the
last two fingers of the hands. When the elbow is acci-
dentally bumped, striking the ulnar nerve, or funny
bone, a numbing sensation is often felt in the last two
fingers of the hand. The relay of nerve sensations often
leads to a temporary loss of feeling to the fingers. In
some forms of martial arts the elbow is used as a point
of leverage for takedown and arm-lock techniques.
Jujitsu and aikido use elbow-lock methods of forcing
an attacker to the ground in more instances than do
most other forms of martial arts. However, elbow lever-

age and locking techniques will be found in the weapon defense techniques of literally every form of unarmed combat in the world, especially for gun and knife defenses.

Figure 113 shows a typical locking system for breaking the elbow. Figure 114 shows a typical opposing force application for takedown purposes for this class V-B target area.

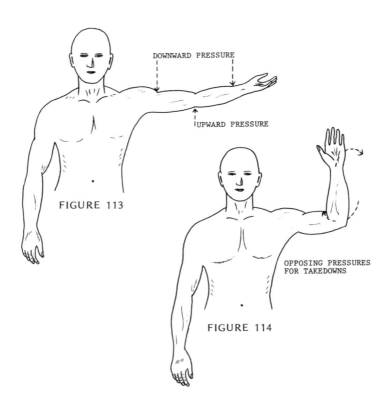

DOWNWARD PRESSURE

UPWARD PRESSURE

FIGURE 113

OPPOSING PRESSURES
FOR TAKEDOWNS

FIGURE 114

Master Long has assumed a left-faced back stance to his opponent's left forward stance.

Having shifted his stance to elude an oncoming high gate punch, Master Long has locked the arm at the elbow. Breaking force or a pain-giving jolt may be applied to the area.

Assuming that the movement has not broken the joint loose, Master Long is applying his body weight and muscle pressure against the elbow, forcing his opponent to the ground.

3. Dragons Strike to the Chest and Abdomen

The ventral medial plane contains pressure points 25 through 34, listed below, a total of ten. It begins beneath the collarbone and extends down to the abdomen, including the front of the arms to the tips of the fingers.

25. Sternum
26. Substernal notch
27. Solar plexus
28. Heart
29. Ribs
30. Abdominal area
31. Biceps
32. Radial nerve
33. Carpus
34. Phalanges

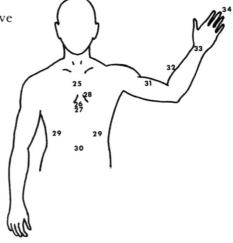

Sternum

As a target area, the sternum (figure 115) is one of the most overlooked pressure points in the body; more-so on a large, strong man's chest, because it is believed that a larger man's chest would be impervious to pain or injury. The fact is that the larger the target, the easier it is to hit. Again, let your own body prove the sensitivity. Form a fist with your hand, but protrude the thumb knuckle by pressing the tip of the thumb against the index finger. Lightly strike your sternum at the center and slowly increase the striking force until you feel the pain. It will not take much pressure to convince you that a full-power strike could be extremely painful.

The sternum is a flat narrow bone about six inches long situated in the centermost line between the pectoralis muscles in the front of the thorax. It develops as three separate parts: the upper manubrium; the middle and largest segment, the gladiolus; and the lower tip, the xiphoid (see figure 116). There are notches on the manubrium and gladiolus for the upper seven ribs. The xiphoid has no ribs attached to it but is attached to some of the abdominal muscles. The structural function of the sternum is to provide reception for the first seven ribs from the thoracic vertebrae, thus helping to form

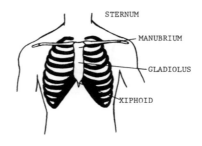

FIGURE 115

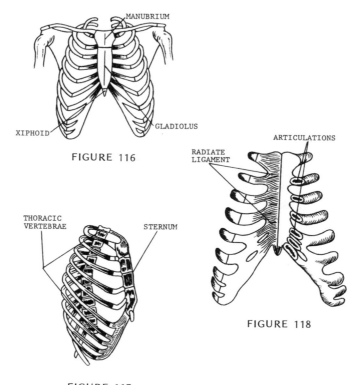

MANUBRIUM

XIPHOID

GLADIOLUS

FIGURE 116

RADIATE LIGAMENT

ARTICULATIONS

FIGURE 118

THORACIC VERTEBRAE

STERNUM

FIGURE 117

the protective enclosure called the thorax around many vital portions of the body, notably the heart and lungs. Figure 117 shows the right side of the thoracic basket. The ribs articulate with the thoracic vertebrae at the posterior formation (refer to pressure points 19 and 20), and with the sternum at the anterior formation of the thorax. The costal cartilages (ribs) join the sternum, fused by the radiate ligaments (figure 118). From the facing view, the left side shows the radiate ligaments, the right side shows the articulations.

As a target area, the sternum furnishes excellent cardiorespiratory response to a thrust. To perform the heart massage used in C.P.R. (see pressure point 11), it is sometimes necessary to break the sternum and push it against the heart with palm pressure for stimulation. This is possible because the heart lies close behind the sternum, and the sternum is easily broken.

Snap contact or shallow penetration to the sternum would be extremely painful. A thrust or deep penetrating blow could cause cardiorespiratory response ranging from pain and coughing to temporary paralysis of the vital organs and unconsciousness. Figure 119 shows the proper directions in which force should be applied. Figure 120 shows the preferred location in which to deliver the strike. The sternum is a class V-A target area.

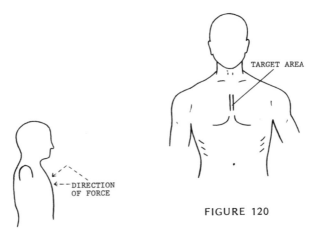

FIGURE 120

FIGURE 119

Master Long assumes a right lead cat position against his opponent's straddle.

His opponent, stepping into a left forward stance, has thrown a reverse punch. Master Long has slightly broken his stance to begin a forward position, using a crossing forearm block. Note that the left hand has been chambered.

Master Long delivers a full vertical punch to the sternum. Note the rotation of the body into the strike.

Substernal Notch

It seems ironic, and almost unbelievable, that one of the most devastating targets in the human anatomy is left relatively unprotected in every form of unarmed combat. On the other hand, knowledge of the angle and the proper penetration are necessary to make the substernal notch the death target it can be.

Several factors are involved in the attack. To begin, figure 121 is a frontal view of the thorax, illustrating the precise location of the heart in relation to the ribs and sternum; take special note of the xiphoid. In figure 116, a more realistic view of the xiphoid is presented. The cartilaginous projection is an attachment to the sternum. Taking in a deep breath, press lightly with your fingers into the area. Then, pressing lightly onto the xiphoid, note the pliability and location with respect to the rib cage. You are touching one of the most deadly targets in the human anatomy. When properly struck, the xiphoid becomes a puncturing instrument

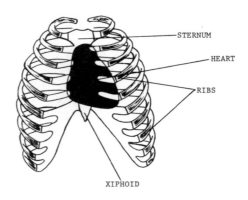

FIGURE 121

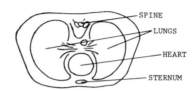

FIGURE 122

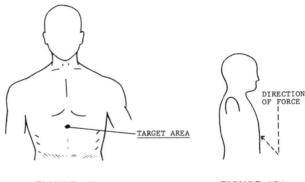

FIGURE 123   FIGURE 124

to the most vital organ in the body—the heart. Referring to figure 122, observe the location of the heart in relation to the sternum and costal cavity. This overhead cutaway view of the thorax depicts how the heart lies almost directly against the sternum. By forcefully striking the xiphoid on a rising 45-degree plane, it can be broken and forced into the heart. The result would, of course, be instantaneous death. It takes deep penetration of the target, coupled with the rising 45-degree angle, to sever the xiphoid and send it into the heart.

Figure 123 depicts the precise location of the target; figure 124 shows the proper angle of attack for this III-D class target area.

Master Long has blocked an attempt to grab his groin.

Here Master Long has grappled the arm of the opponent at the wrist, countering with a ball kick to the substernal notch. It may seem unbelievable, but contacting the substernal notch correctly with a ball kick could very easily be fatal. Power and angle of attack are key factors.

Solar Plexus

To properly understand this pressure point and the effects of striking it, two basic contact centers must be analyzed. To begin, the solar plexus is described as the epigastric and also the celiac plexus. The term *solar plexus* refers to the nerve network supplying all the viscera in the abdominal cavity. In this network exists a multitude of nerves and ganglia, as well as nine other nerve plexuses. The nerve mass surrounds the celiac trunk and mesenteric artery (figure 125). This area

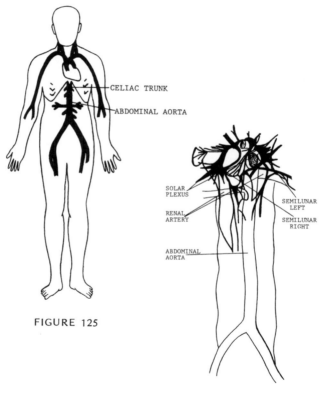

FIGURE 125

FIGURE 126

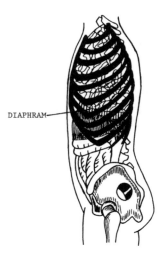

DIAPHRAM

FIGURE 127

should not be confused with the substernal notch,
chiefly because the striking results are extremely different. The principal ganglia of the solar plexus are the
two semilunar ganglia located on either side of the
plexus. They are the largest ganglia in the body and represent the basis of the attack for this pressure point.
Figure 126 is an illustration of the nerves of the solar
plexus and some of the connecting branches to other
plexuses of the body. Structurally, the solar plexus is
situated in front of the diaphragm, on the central face
of the thorax. The side skeletal view in figure 127 illustrates the location of the diaphragm in the body, which
leads into the second contact point of this nerve center.
At the costal cartilages, the muscular fibers of the diaphragm are deficient. The spaces are filled with areolar
tissue and are therefore weaker areas. When a rupture

occurs, the intestines could protrude into the chest, forming a hernia that would require surgical correction. Effecting such a rupture requires deep penetration of the blow. A lesser application of force would cause contraction of the diaphragm, expelling the air in the lungs and resulting in the "winding" effect. The lesser force would also cause abdominal pain from the contact to the semilunar ganglia of the solar plexus. Cramping throughout the abdominal cavity would occur for a short period, accompanied by difficulty in resuming a normal breathing pattern. Unconsciousness often accompanies these symptoms for a brief period. Figure 128 shows the precise area where force should be applied. Figures 129 and 130 show the proper angles at which to apply force to this class IV-C target area.

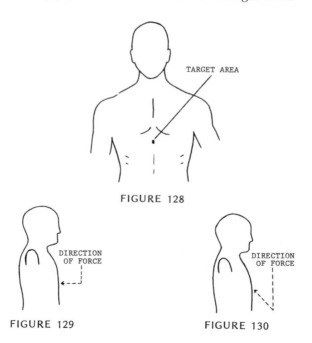

TARGET AREA

FIGURE 128

DIRECTION OF FORCE

DIRECTION OF FORCE

FIGURE 129

FIGURE 130

Here, Master Long's opponent has taken a crane-form modification in preparation for quick attack.

The opponent has attempted a heel thrust at Master Long's knee. He first squats to reinforce the quadriceps into the knee, and then blocks with a sweeping palm block.

Retaining the leg by grappling the ankle, Master Long slides into a kneeling forward position and delivers a vertical palm strike to the solar plexus. Note the slight incline of the attack, unlike the substernal notch attack depicted in the "Planes" chapter of this book.

Heart

It is not necessary to detail the function of the heart with respect to life. The heart maintains the circulation of blood throughout the body. When it stops, life stops. To directly contact the heart would be difficult, since it is well protected within the thorax by the ribs and sternum, as illustrated in figure 131. However, because the heart lies close to these protective shields (see figure 122), they can be used as shock-transfer mechanisms or cutting and puncturing devices. (See pressure point 26.) Figure 131 shows the approximate location of the heart in relation to the thorax. Note that the majority of its mass lies to the left of the center line of the chest; therefore, attacks to the heart should be directed to this area.

In the martial arts, different strikes have different effects. Some are used for deep penetration, while others are used for a shallow and cutting effect. Some are used to produce a vibrative or concussion effect to

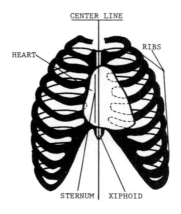

FIGURE 131

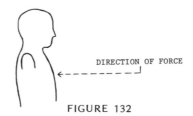

DIRECTION OF FORCE

FIGURE 132

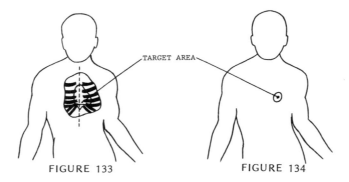

TARGET AREA

FIGURE 133   FIGURE 134

the target. Good examples are the advancing side kick
and the roundhouse kick. The advancing side kick is
a driving, deep penetration attack, while the roundhouse
kick is a snapping concussion blow. The latter is used
for attacking the heart. Vibrative strikes utilizing "snap"
movements are most effective in attacking the heart
because shock is the key to the attack, as in attacking
the tip of the mandible (pressure point 10). The deep
penetration blow to the heart can be effective when a
stomp is used to attack an opponent who is lying on the
ground face-up.

The heart is classed III-C or III-D, according to the
force applied. Figures 132-134 illustrate direction and
the target location.

Master Long and his opponent are in opposing positions, both in right lead stances.

The opponent has attempted a sliding ball kick at groin level, and Master Long has executed a downward suto block while simultaneously cocking the right side of his body for the return strike.

With full rotation of the hips, shoulders, and stance, Master Long delivers a full vertical punch to the heart.

Ribs

In pressure point 20, the ribs were discussed with reference to the posterior view of the torso. Reference here is to the anterior portion of the torso, figure 135. There are a total of twenty-four ribs in the body, twelve pairs joined by the vertebral column at the rear, and by the sternum and costal cartilages in front. There are twelve ribs on each side of the thorax, connected by a thoracic vertebra by the head and tubercle of the

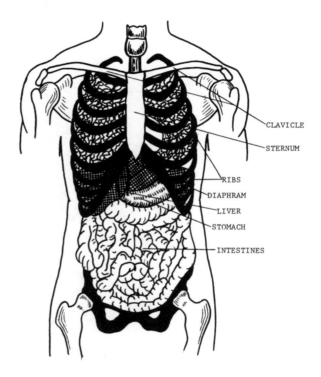

FIGURE 135

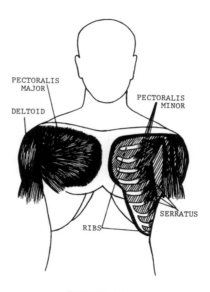

FIGURE 136

posterior extremity. The head fits into a facet formed on the body of one vertebra, or formed by the adjacent bodies of two vertebrae; the tubercle articulates with the transverse process. Strong ligaments surround and bind these articulations but permit slight gliding movements. A full view from the side showing the sternal and vertebral articulations can be found in figure 84.

Attacking the ribs from the front involves a problem analogous to that of striking the ribs from the rear. The pectoralis major and minor muscles protect all but the sixth through tenth ribs. Figure 136 shows a cutaway view of the upper chest, the left side showing pectoralis major and the right side showing pectoralis minor. As can be seen in the illustration, the remaining five ribs are unprotected and lie indirectly against the lungs. Striking these ribs will cause the winding effect with medium pressure, and, of course, maximum striking force could easily break them. It is important to focus the strike onto the last five ribs (sixth through tenth) because the floating ribs cannot be struck from the front.

There are several angles that can be used to focus pressure on the ribs. A rising 45-degree strike could be more deadly because it increases the chance of snapping a rib and forcing it into a lung. A horizontal strike may yield the same results, but the likelihood is greater with the rising attack. Horizontal angles can also vary. Figure 137 shows some variations. Figure 138 shows the vertical and horizontal applications. The ribs are a class V-B target area.

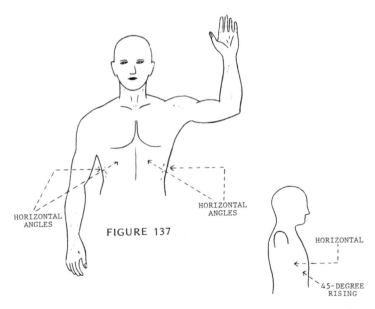

FIGURE 137

FIGURE 138

Master Long and his opponent are again in opposing stances.

His opponent attempts an overhand punch to the head. Master Long has stepped away and begins the spinning movement of his next maneuver.

In completing the technique, Master Long has rotated 180 degrees and delivered a spinning side kick focused at the ribs.

Abdominal Area

It would be best to review pressure point 27, the solar plexus, before continuing the abdominal study. As figure 139 illustrates, the abdominal muscles meet and join at the lower ribs and xiphoid at the solar plexus area, and above the groin in the lower extremity. Abdominal muscles function to protect the abdominal organs, ventrally flex the spinal column, and contract the diaphragm.

Strengthening and hardening the abdominals is practiced extensively in combat sports and in other competitive sports as well. It is a large area and often very weak in the average person today. Many times a good punch in the stomach will send an opponent to the floor, doubled up in pain and out of breath; but to assume that such an easily developed area as the abdo-

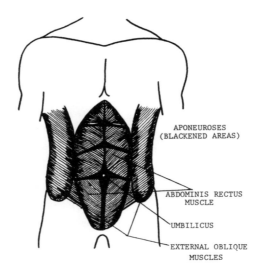

APONEUROSES
(BLACKENED AREAS)

ABDOMINIS RECTUS
MUSCLE

UMBILICUS

EXTERNAL OBLIQUE
MUSCLES

FIGURE 139

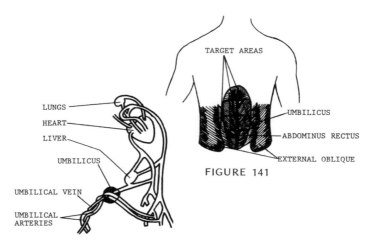

TARGET AREAS

LUNGS

HEART

LIVER

UMBILICUS

UMBILICAL VEIN

UMBILICAL
ARTERIES

UMBILICUS

ABDOMINUS RECTUS

EXTERNAL OBLIQUE

FIGURE 141

FIGURE 140

men is going to be weak in the attacker you face is
foolish and very dangerous. Therefore, the area is analyzed here to reveal its weakest points.

As illustrated in figure 139, there are actually four
pairs of muscles joined by aponeuroses, or connective
tissue, that form the abdominal group. Each of these
aponeuroses represents a weaker area. In three of the
aponeuroses, weaknesses are found, caused by the protrusion of organic tubes into lower anatomical organs.
These are the inguinal canals, femoral rings, and umbilicus. Our attention is focused on the umbilicus, for
its total weakened area is the greatest and most accessible for attack. The umbilicus, more commonly
referred to as the navel, is a nonfunctional aperture in
adult life, closed since birth, and existing as an aponeurosis in the abdomen. Before birth, the umbilicus was a
passage through which nourishment and oxygen were
conveyed to the fetus from the placenta by means of
the umbilical cord. In figure 140, an illustration of the
umbilicus displays the blood tracts which permitted life

before birth, and shows the three blood tracts which now exist as a weakened area in the abdominal group. The blood lines, needless to say, are no longer needed. They are cut off at birth and form what is now referred to as the navel. In this area, where the muscles join the umbilicus, exists a portion of connective tissue which closes the area and joins the muscles (figure 141). This abdominal area is weaker than the areas more closely fused and is therefore the basic target for the abdominal attack.

Referring back to figure 138, areas denoted by arrows are secondary focus points, due to the unattached joining of the external oblique muscle and the abdominus rectus muscle. Considering the off-center position of these focus points, they are valuable as target areas because, unlike the umbilicus, they can be attacked at an angle with full-force concentration of the blow without direct alignment with the vital center line. This attack would penetrate even a well-developed abdomen because it is focused between the muscle formations and not directly on one or the other.

Figure 141 illustrates the target areas. Figures 142 and 143 show the proper angles of attack. Pressure point 30 is a class III-B target area.

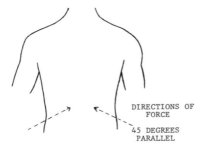

DIRECTIONS OF
FORCE

45 DEGREES
PARALLEL

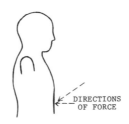

DIRECTIONS
OF FORCE

FIGURE 142   FIGURE 143

Master Long is gripped by a two-handed choke from the front.

Here Master Long has broken the arms in a downward motion with forearm strikes, using the blocking area of the arms against the opponent's radial nerve on each arm. The right leg is also cocked in preparation for a front kick.

In the final movement, Master Long has thrust a ball kick to the umbilicus. Because the opponent is in a forward position, leaning over from the arm strike, the proper angle of attack is achieved by a 45-degree incline.

Biceps

The function of the biceps (figure 144) is to close
the arm laterally; when resistance is used, it controls
the opening of the arm when vertically positioned. Since
its function is to raise or pull toward the body, the
biceps is more commonly used in everyday life than
many other muscles. In figure 145, the biceps muscles
are shown, displaying the origin and insertion points,

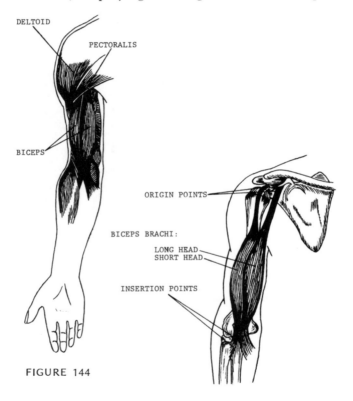

FIGURE 144

FIGURE 145

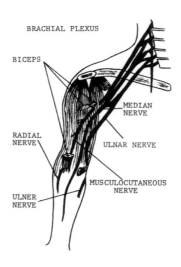

FIGURE 146

and also illustrating that the formation is actually two different muscles. There are other smaller muscles that assist in the lateral movement, but our attention will be focused on the biceps. Since the biceps controls a large portion of the movement of the radius (forearm), the operation of the biceps is fundamentally critical in blocking and striking with the hands and arms. Turn back to pressure points 13 and 17, the brachial plexus. In figure 146, note that the musculocutaneous nerve, the median nerve, and the radial nerves are all branches of the brachial plexus, and these nerves continue down into the lower arm. Just as striking the brachial plexus can paralyze the entire limb from the shoulder down, attacking the musculocutaneous nerve and the median nerve can paralyze the arm from the biceps down. The muscles contain nerve fibers which, when struck, could be extremely painful and disabling, although the main branches lie beneath the muscle formation. Contacting the main branches would be more likely to cause paralysis. Without the operation of the biceps, the arm cannot be held in a folded position for protective purposes, and, of course, blocking and striking with the affected arm is out of the question.

The biceps will fall under the numerical class IV, muscular functions and nerves, but it should be noted that it is equally a class V target area because the results inhibit the use of a mechanical function. We will classify the target as IV-A for the purpose of this book. Figure 147 shows the precise target area. Figures 148 and 149 show the proper angles of attack.

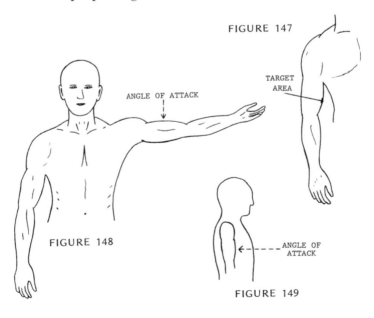

FIGURE 147

TARGET AREA

ANGLE OF ATTACK

FIGURE 148

ANGLE OF ATTACK

FIGURE 149

Master Long is grabbed by the lapel by the opponent's right hand.

Master Long has grabbed the opponent's hand by placing his four fingers around the muscles of the thumb and placing his thumb on the last bone of the outside of the hand at the top.

With a slight jerking motion to release the opponent's grip and turn the biceps up, Master Long follows through with an overhand suto to the biceps. Additional strikes should be used as finishing technique.

Radial Nerve

Most of the groundwork for the radial nerve is set forth in pressure point 31, the biceps. The radial nerve is a branch of the musculocutaneous nerve, which originates from the brachial plexus at the cervical colum (see figure 146). The value of this target does not match that of the biceps. Although the degree of pain is relatively similar, there is no loss of mechanical function. A strike to the radial nerve, however, would be extremely painful, as you can easily demonstrate to yourself. Stiffen

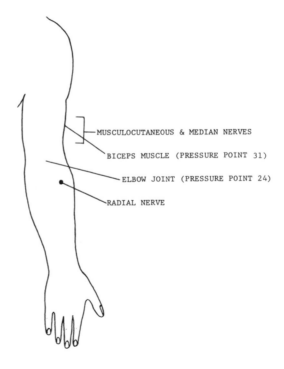

MUSCULOCUTANEOUS & MEDIAN NERVES

BICEPS MUSCLE (PRESSURE POINT 31)

ELBOW JOINT (PRESSURE POINT 24)

RADIAL NERVE

FIGURE 150

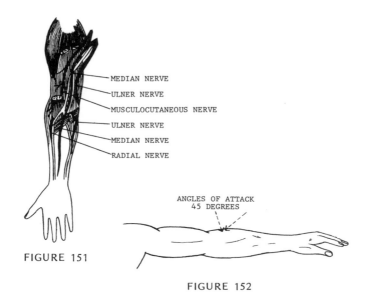

FIGURE 151

FIGURE 152

your left index finger and lay your right arm, palm down, on a flat surface. Travel down the pit of the arm at the biceps about two inches and across the arm about one inch. Feel around for the sensitive spot and poke it lightly (figure 150). As you can see, the radial nerve is even very sensitive to lightly applied pressure.

Figure 151 illustrates the radial nerve as it surfaces from beneath the biceps (short head) at the insertion point in the forearm. The radial nerve is mentioned in this text for its availability as a target in countering grabs and in blocking, but it would not be practical to focus an attack on this area in a standoff situation unless the arm has been blocked and grabbed.

Figure 150 shows the approximate location of the focal point; figure 152 illustrates the proper angle of attack. The radial nerve is a class IV-A target area.

Master Long is in a right lead cat position. His opponent is in a similar position, but is poised for a short right-hand punch.

Having blocked the advancing punch with an outer forearm block from the inside, Master Long grapples the arm at the wrist and cocks a suto strike and body position.

In the completed movement, Master Long's suto has landed on the radial nerve of his opponent's right arm. Again take note that the hips, stance, and shoulders have rotated in the direction of the blow.

Carpus

The carpus, or wrist, is composed of eight small bones joined by ligaments. They are arranged in two rows and lie close together. The carpus is classified as a gliding joint; it allows the circular movement of the hand.

As illustrated in figures 153 and 154, the wrist is powered by four muscles located in the radial arm. The radial arm, or forearm, can be made extremely powerful though proper training, but the many small bones of the carpus make it nearly impossible to strengthen it totally against wrist locks and wrist lever throws. Figure 155 is a close-up skeletal view of the right hand. The eight bones that join to form the carpus are illustrated and named. Its restricted motion capacity makes it easy to lock and apply painful pressure to the joint.

Nearly every martial art incorporates joint-pressure techniques in one facet of training or another. Most commonly, wrist and elbow pressure will be found in the weapon defense techniques and in countering grap-

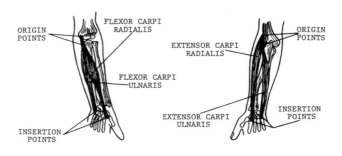

FIGURE 153   FIGURE 154

ples; the most prevalent are one- and two-hand chokes and lapel grabs. It would be wise to remember that in applying these pressure techniques, snap-to-lock and hold pressure will be more effective than the steadily increasing pressure to a submission point. The carpus is classified as a V-A target. The accompanying photographs illustrate some common locking applications.

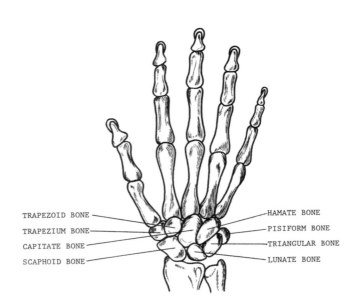

TRAPEZOID BONE —   —HAMATE BONE
TRAPEZIUM BONE—   —PISIFORM BONE
CAPITATE BONE—   —TRIANGULAR BONE
SCAPHOID BONE—   — LUNATE BONE

FIGURE 155

Upon being grabbed by the wrist, Master Long immediately strikes his opponent in the throat to divert his attention and weaken his grip.

The hand is grabbed by four fingers around the muscle of the thumb and twisted to release the grip.

After breaking the grip, Master Long places his other hand on the other side of the opponent's hand and bends the wrist toward the arm. By kneeling, the pressure is increased and the opponent is now controlled.

Here Master Long is grabbed by the collar.

He steps slightly forward, grasping the hand in the same manner and delivering a vertical punch to the lower ribs at the same time.

This time the wrist is kept high and twisted clockwise, putting pressure on the joint above the wrist.

Phalanges

Very little time will be spent on this pressure point. Figure 155 illustrates the skeletal structures of the hand and fingers; figure 112 in Chapter 2 shows the nerve tract from the brachial plexus down to the fingertips. Fingers are easily broken when leverage is used against the knuckles. Although a broken finger or two can be very painful, you should not expect such an injury to stop a serious attacker.

The great value of the phalanges as pressure points is in breaking holds. A broken finger cannot function to maintain a grip. You can usually peel off one finger at a time rather easily, and if every time you peel one off you snap it, it won't take long to get your point across to whoever is trying to keep a grip on you. It is best to begin with the fifth, or little, finger, as it is the smallest and most easily peeled loose.

As was pointed out in pressure point 33, a steadily increasing power is suitable for practice, but not for the streets, where a snapping full-pressure application is advisable.

The accompanying photographs will demonstrate some basic locking and breaking techniques for this V-B class target area.

Master Long has been grabbed by the neck from behind, and has begun a peeling technique to pry his opponent's grip loose from his neck. One finger only from each hand should be grabbed. This will focus the greatest amount of pressure onto the minimum receiving surface, the same principle used in focusing the first two knuckles into a punch.

The opponent's fingers have been pried loose and could easily have been broken off by applying a snap movement. Instead, the slowly increasing pressure is used for demonstration and practice purposes.

4. Dragons Strike to the Groin and Legs

The ventral caudal plane consists of the front portion of the legs from the groin to the feet. There are a total of six pressure points cited in Chapter 4, starting with number 35 and ending with number 40.

35. Groin
36. Anterior femoral region
37. Patella
38. Knee joints
39. Tibia
40. Tarsus

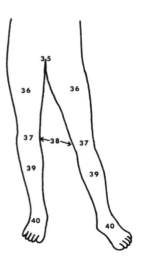

Groin

The most sensitive area of the groin is the glandular formation called the testes (figure 156). They are classified as compound tubular glands because they open into an excretory duct, the urethral opening at the end of the penis. The primary function of the testes is reproductive, but they also assist in the development and maintenance of male secondary sex characteristics.

The exceptional sensitivity of the testes is common knowledge to the majority of adult males. As a target area, the scrotum, which houses the testes, is valuable, not only for its sensitivity, but also for its anatomical location. It may be noted that the application of striking force is markedly different than for other pressure points. Both light and heavy contacts seem to produce more effective results than medium contact. A very hard

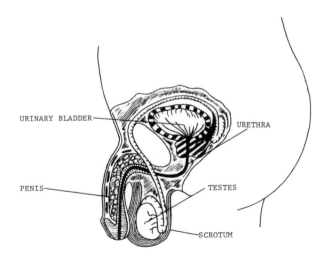

FIGURE 156

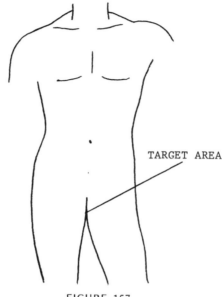

TARGET AREA

FIGURE 157

strike could, of course, cause structural damage requiring surgical correction or perhaps amputation, but through experience I find that a light slap is more painful than a medium-force blow. A very hard blow, however, is more painful.

A groin strike is often temporarily disabling, due to the transmission of pain into the abdominal area. The pain is often accompanied by nausea and abdominal cramping. Although the effects of a groin strike are extremely painful and frequently temporarily disabling, this target should be attacked in combination with other pressure points and not relied upon to take an opponent down or keep him down. Groin strikes in some cases are effective psychologically as well as physically. Most men have a greater fear of being struck in the groin than in

the nose; yet, if you refer back to pressure point 7, you
will see that a blow to the nose can be much more dangerous. A strike to the nose can be deadly, while a strike
of equal force to the groin will not be fatal. Unless the
blow is exceptionally powerful or made with a cutting
instrument, a strike to the groin is not lethal.

The target area is illustrated in figure 157. The
angles of attack are illustrated in figure 158. The groin is
a class IV-A target area.

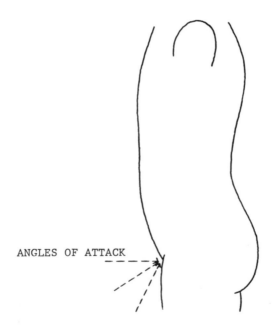

ANGLES OF ATTACK

FIGURE 158

Master Long and his opponent are in opposing positions.

Having feinted his head forward to draw a high-section punch, Master Long has dropped to one knee and strikes and grabs his opponent's groin.

To complete the movement, Master Long follows through with his counterattack by applying arm, shoulder, and body tension to effect a maximum power rip of the groin.

Anterior Femoral Region

The anterior femoral region is the area between the hip joint and the knee on the face side of the body in front of the femur. This pressure point was named in a more general description because three specific target areas will be cited.

The first two are in the quadriceps femoris muscle group. Depicted individually in figures 159 through 162, the quadriceps is a four-muscle group, consisting of rectus femoris, vastus intermedius, vastus medialis, and vastus lateralis. These four muscles form the quadriceps, a powerful lever for the knee joint which permits the development of the devastating leg extension kicks, such as the side kick and the roundhouse kick. The quadriceps femoris also facilitates the ability to stand, which

FIGURE 159

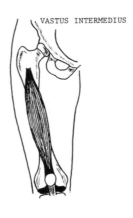

FIGURE 160

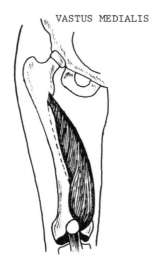

VASTUS MEDIALIS

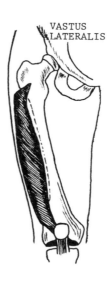

VASTUS LATERALIS

FIGURE 161   FIGURE 162

gives it its value as a combat target. An effective attack on the vastus medialis or vastus lateralis, trapping the muscle between the anatomical weapon and the femur bone, would have a crippling spasmodic effect, immobilizing the afflicted leg. To structurally immobilize an opponent may be the only feasible way to stop him at a given moment, and this capability should be sought by every martial artist. This of course excludes attacking lethal targets.

The third and final focal point is a direct nerve attack. The anterior cutaneous nerve is located in the upper and outer surfaces of the rectus femoris muscle (see figure 163). It is a branch of the femoral nerve, a main body supplying the leg. In contacting this focal point, the nerve is hit directly and would therefore afford greater pain response.

These three target areas should be attacked with maximum force to yield an immobilizing effect. Target locations are shown in figure 164. The angles of attack are illustrated in figure 165. The anterior femoral region is a class IV-A target area.

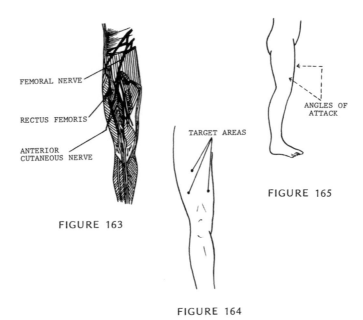

FEMORAL NERVE

RECTUS FEMORIS

ANTERIOR
CUTANEOUS NERVE

FIGURE 163

TARGET AREAS

FIGURE 164

ANGLES OF
ATTACK

FIGURE 165

Master Long has assumed a crane variation in preparation for his defensive maneuver.

In meeting his opponent's oncoming punch, Master Long has redirected the blow upward with a palm block and thrust his heel into the anterior femoral region.

In following through with the counterattack, the opponent is knocked off balance in addition to the physical result of the attack.

Patella and Knee Joint

Pressure points 37 and 38, the patella and the knee joint, will be examined together, due to their immediate proximity to each other.

Of all the pressure points in the body, the knee joint and patella represent the last target that should be forgotten, and the first target that should be struck as a lead. In most cases, the knee is the most readily available, the least protected, and the most unexpected target. Yet structurally, mechanically, and defensively, it is the number one pressure point for a counterattack in every aspect of a "must do" defensive situation, for several reasons:

1. As a target, the knee is anatomically positioned where the most powerful muscles may be used in the attack, assisted by body weight and gravity, with a downward side kick.

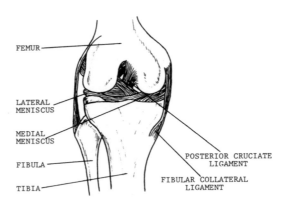

FIGURE 166

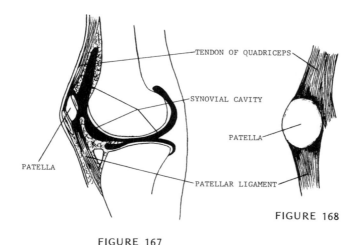

FIGURE 167

FIGURE 168

2. The knee is more difficult to protect than pressure points within the range of the hand-arm span.

3. An effective attack to the knee destroys the nucleus of physical combat-balance.

4. An effective attack to the knee destroys locomotion and support.

The sides of the knee and the patella, or kneecap, are the focus points of the attack, but it is the ligaments that suffer the destruction. The knee joint's basic structural strength relies on fourteen ligaments which bind the articulation together. Figure 165 is a front view of the knee showing articulation of the femur, fibula, and tibia and some of the connective ligaments (patella removed). The knee is a hinge class joint in which there is no horizontal movement. The knee locks into a straight line in its fully opened position. Pressure should be applied to stress these limits in their respective directions.

In figure 167, the knee is viewed internally from the side showing articular cartilage and the synovial membrane. The free movement of the patella is permitted by the synovial cavity, and also, as figure 168 illustrates, the patellar confinement is applied only at the upper and lower vertical ends. Horizontal movement is therefore comparatively unrestricted.

There are a number of ways to attack the knee joint and the patella, and there are an assortment of effective angles at which force may be concentrated, making this focus point a valuable target area for learning and practicing attack techniques. The utmost caution should be used in practicing such techniques, for you can count on a knee injury to set back your training for a year.

Figure 169 illustrates the basic focus points; figures 170 and 171 display the multiple directions in which force may be applied. The patella and knee joint are classified as V-B target areas.

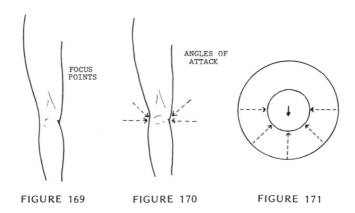

FIGURE 169   FIGURE 170   FIGURE 171

Master Long's opponent has drawn a club for the attack. Note that in his defensive position, Master Long has exposed the side of his head facing the weapon. This is done to draw the attack to that area.

The opponent, seeing the side of the head unprotected, attempts to land a strike to the area. Because the weapon is being swung at a 45-degree angle at the head, the arm and weapon can be avoided by ducking down and away from the arc of the swing. Master Long has simultaneously cocked his left leg for his counterattack.

In the completed move, the weapon has passed safely over Master Long's head, which he has pulled far away from the danger area; in so doing he provides a strong counterweight for his thrusting side kick to the patella.

The side of the knee is a target of supreme value, and here Master Long has taken position for a side kick to the knee.

With a wrist block, Master Long executes a devastating low side kick to the side of the knee. In immobilizing a leg, a mechanical function is taken away from the opponent, along with balance and the ability to stand evenly on the legs or to maneuver.

Tibia

The tibia is the larger of the two bones located vertically between the knee and the ankle, more commonly known as the shinbone. Everyone has at one time or another experienced the shocking and intense pain of smacking a shinbone on a ledge, a chair, an open drawer, or some such obstruction. A detailed description of the pain response is not necessary, but to be blunt, it's excruciating.

The shin is so sensitive because, like the cranium, the clavicle, and the posterior point of the elbow, the bone is relatively exposed, covered only by skin. The muscular tracts of the lower leg leave the tibia exposed at the center and inside angles, leaving a cherry of a target for heels and hard-tipped shoes. The tibia's real value as a target is in grappling situations when the arms are pinned. The tibia can be struck with a back-thrusting heel kick, or raked from the knee down, ending in a stomp to the tarsus.

The tibia is a class V-A target area. The precise target location is depicted in figure 172. The angles of attack are depicted in figure 173.

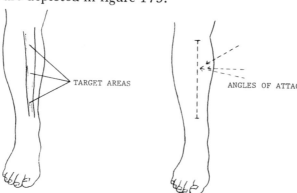

TARGET AREAS

ANGLES OF ATTACK

FIGURE 172   FIGURE 173

Here Master Long is grabbed by two hands around the neck from the front—a serious position to be in. He grabs the opponent's arms, raising his right leg to deliver a kick.

A crossing heel kick is delivered to the opponent's tibia. This is a good method of beginning a hold-breaking technique. Other blows should follow.

Being held by the neck from the front by one hand, Master Long takes hold of the attacking hand and the jaw of his opponent. His right leg is raised in preparation for a kick.

Here Master Long delivers a side kick to his opponent's tibia. Notice the hip position in relation to the preceding photograph.

Maintaining his grip on the hand and on the jaw, Master Long rakes the edge of his foot down the face of the tibia and stomps the top of the foot.

Tarsus

The tarsus—the collection of bones between the tibia and the metatarsus—although a very sensitive target area, is, strangely enough, one of the most powerful anatomical weapons of the body. The first metatarsal articulation to the phalanx is the ball of the foot, used as a focus point for the front ball kick and the round-house ball kick. The cuneiform and metatarsal groups forming the upper surface of the foot are used in the bridge kick, and the calcaneus is used to focus the side and thrust kicks. As strange as it may seem, however, the majority of the tarsus serves well as a target area.

Much like pressure point 39, the tarsus becomes a practical target in grappling situations or in close confinement where available fighting space is very limited. It should be noted that a blow delivered to the tarsus can be as structurally disabling as an attack to the knee. The tarsus is a supportive structure, and when standing on the foot is extremely painful, structural disability has in fact been achieved.

Figure 174 is a schematic of the bone structure of this target area. Figure 175 shows the focus point and angle of attack. The tarsus is a class V-B target area.

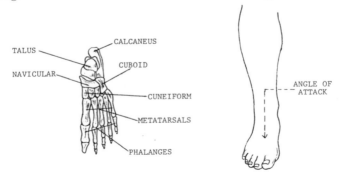

FIGURE 174   FIGURE 175

This is an example of using the bridge of the foot in close-range technique. The foot has been stomped and is also being held in place, restricting defensive movements of the opponent.

Master Long is stomping the foot as he begins a peel-off and wrist-lock technique.

Master Long eliminates the possibility of his opponent's retreat as he strikes the groin with a backhand.

5. Dragons Strike to the Coccyx and Legs

The dorsal caudal plane comprises the rear portion of the legs from the coccyx to the feet. There are a total of three pressure points cited in Chapter 5 (41 through 43). This is the last anatomical group to be discussed.

41. Coccyx
42. Tibial nerve
43. Gastrocnemius muscle

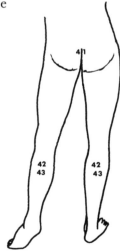

Coccyx

The crucial function performed by the vertebral column need not be explored at this time. It has been discussed extensively in this text in pressure points 16, 18, and 19. Nerve impulses from the brain are transmitted through and distributed by the spinal cord, the core of the vertebral column. At the dorsal tip, the coccyx emerges at the medial posterior portion of the hip girdle (figure 176; see also figure 84). A blow of sufficient force to the coccyx would be instantly paralyzing. Neurological response would reach the tip of every limb and into the pons; see pressure point 10. If the striking force is sufficient to structurally damage the bone formation, permanent paralysis can result.

The surface location of the coccyx and the angles of attack are illustrated in figure 177 for this IV-B target area.

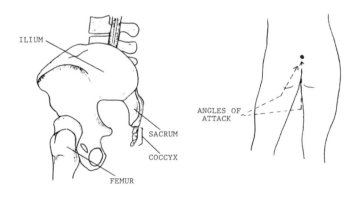

FIGURE 176   FIGURE 177

Master Long is leading the attack from behind. In his first move he grapples the head and the base of the neck in a forward stance in preparation for his next movement.

The head and neck are tightly held and pulled slightly back, while the knee is thrust into the coccyx.

Tibial Nerve and Gastrocnemius Muscle

The posterior tibial nerve is located at the center-most point of the calf. It emerges as a branch of the great sciatic nerve in the posterior femoral region and branches down behind the knee as the tibial nerve running vertically down into the heel of the foot (figure 178). The nerve lies on the surface of the deep muscles and is covered by the gastrocnemius muscle; see figure 179. The gastrocnemius muscle controls the extension of the foot, making it possible to walk in a smooth motion, to run, and perform similar movements. It is

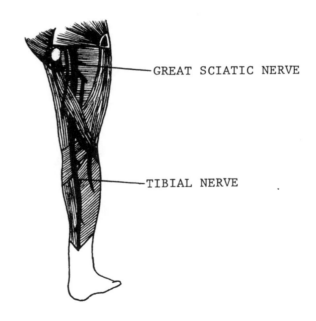

GREAT SCIATIC NERVE

TIBIAL NERVE

FIGURE 178

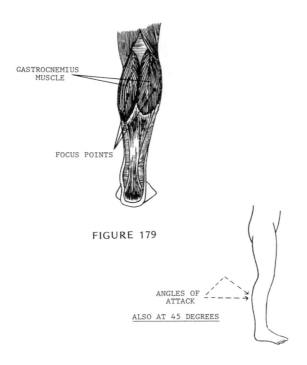

GASTROCNEMIUS
MUSCLE

FOCUS POINTS

FIGURE 179

ANGLES OF
ATTACK
ALSO AT 45 DEGREES

FIGURE 180

sensitive to attack due to the fibrous communication with the tibial nerve, mostly at the outer portions of its form.

These pressure points should not be considered primary target areas. Although the pain resulting from an effective strike to these areas can be extensive, the results may not be serious enough to stop an assault. The targets should be used in combination at the angles shown in figure 180. The gastrocnemius muscle and the tibial nerve are class IV-A target areas.

Master Long is taking a step into a cross stance, but instead of completing the stance, he retains his balance on his left leg and delivers a low-hook kick to the tibial nerve. A kick of sufficient force would result in a sweeping result, as well as pain, shown in the photo below.

6. Dragons Strike to Kill

Do you have the right to kill? A serious question, to put it mildly. It really depends on the circumstances and who is answering the question. A basic answer can be found in the preface, but in making the final decision, most people would hesitate. If possible, structurally immobilizing an opponent should be the first choice in a defensive situation, but you should achieve the mental and physical ability to kill. When you are defending yourself against multiple assailants, you may not have the time to execute a combination or go out of your way *not* to kill, and to make that time could mean your life or making the critical list at the hospital. In defense against an armed attacker or multiple armed attackers, debating whether you can or cannot kill, is put aside: You must always preserve your life. If you are in this situation and intend to defend yourself while trying not to hurt anyone, then you are being impractical. Such impracticality could cost you your life.

It is your instructor's responsibility to bring out your self-respect as well as your respect for others, self-love as well as love for others, to bring forth the ferocity of the beast as well as the gentleness of the lamb. When attacked, you must become the fiery dragon of death, not the sacrificial lamb. When the bridge of peace is crossed by evil, meet it with all the mental and physical power you possess. Destroy it before you are destroyed. Think about how and to what degree you will protect yourself and make your decision, because there will be no time to think when someone jumps out from behind a car with a knife or a baseball bat. *You must be prepared mentally.*

In the following photographs, one killing technique is illustrated for each of the five planes, using the respective plane as a lead for a combination or a single counterattack. These techniques should be practiced over and over for speed and accuracy, and for power.

Frame One

Master Long has positioned himself to protect his lifeline as his opponent stands prepared to attack him with a knife.

The opponent thrusts the knife at Master Long's throat, who blocks with an inside suto block and simultaneously executes a finger jab to the eyes.

Retaining the grip he has taken on the attacking arm, Master Long turns the wrist up in preparation for his next move.

Master Long rotates his body and slams a suto hand across the center of the opponent's biceps.

Without stopping, the hand is redirected from its target to its next target in a chicken-wrist form to the temple.

A hard elbow strike is delivered to the radial nerve.

Here Master Long snaps the elbow joint by holding the arm firmly in place and bringing up the knee.

By forcing the opponent's body forward, his head is now within easy reach.

With his hands firmly tightened around the opponent's head, Master Long is now prepared for his final technique.

With a pull of the left hand and a push of the right in sequence, Master Long's opponent is on his way to the floor with a broken cervical column.

Frame Two

As his opponent approaches with a club, Master Long sets his stance wide and exposes the back of his head in an attempt to draw the attack to that area.

The opponent now attempts to land a blow at a 45-degree angle to Master Long's head. Keeping his head back and dropping the parry hand, Master Long begins his countermove.

Guiding the weapon safely past his head by grappling the wrist, Master Long rises to a standing position and begins his attack.

With a full twist and body rotation to propel his strike, Master Long has planted a heel into the thoracic vertebrae.

The opponent has dropped the weapon as Master Long sets his foot down and prepares his next attack.

Having set himself solidly on the ground, Master Long delivers a second blow to the thoracic vertebrae.

Dropping down to his left knee, Master Long reaches between his opponent's legs through to the groin and grabs it tight.

With a final squeeze and a twist, Master Long pulls his arm back as hard as he can, tearing the scrotum.

Master Long now brings up his left foot and grapples the opponent at the collar and the groin.

With a lunge from the back and the legs, Master Long boosts his attacker high in the air, retaining his grip for his final move.

Assisted by the pull of gravity, Master Long pulls his opponent to the ground, meeting him with a supported knee focused at the center of the back.

Frame Three

Master Long's opponent has drawn a knife and is poised to attack.

Having had a thrust made at his throat, Master Long has advanced with his block, keeping a good distance from the weapon.

With a hand-heel strike across the fingers and a chicken-wrist clamp on the back side of the opponent's wrist, Master Long sends the knife flying through the air, disarming his attacker. The knife is the darkened blur outside the opponent's right arm.

Raking the eyes as he steps away, Master Long is now in position for his final blow, cocked fully for maximum impact.

With a full rotation of the power elements and a 45-degree inclining strike to the sub-sternal notch, Master Long's opponent will be dead before he hits the floor.

Frame Four

Here Master Long is being
attacked by an armed sen-
try who has drawn his sword.
He has exposed the left side of
his head to attract the attack
to that area.

The sentry has taken the bait
and swung at his head. All
in one motion, Master Long
drops to one knee and thrusts
a side kick deep into the front
of the knee at the patella.

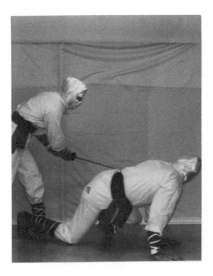

Before the sentry can recover from his swing to execute another attack, Master Long has rotated his body to the opposite knee in preparation for his final technique.

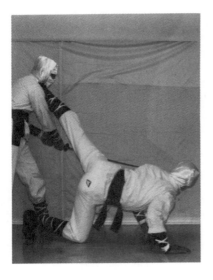

Incorporating the rotation to the opposite knee with a push upward with the hands to add to the impact, Master Long finishes his maneuver with a full-snapping side kick to the sentry's anterior neck region. Unable to breathe through the collapsed windpipe and drowning in his own blood, the sentry will die in seconds.

Frame Five

Master Long is approaching a sentry from behind. He squats low directly behind the sentry, so as not to enter his field of peripheral vision.

His first maneuver is taking the sentry off his feet by delivering a deep-thrusting side kick high on the gastrocnemius muscle. This will bring his final target into easy reach of his hands as the sentry falls onto one knee.

The sentry begins to rotate his body, thus keeping one foot on the ground as he draws his sword. Master Long is already too close and is comfortably positioned on his feet, braced behind the sentry as his hands move into position to grapple the head.

Master Long is well in control as his hands are firmly bound around his target's head to begin his final movement.

The completed movement was, of course, a full-twisting snap of the neck. The sentry is unable to move or speak, his major organs are in a state of arrest, and he will die within seconds.

Conclusion

If you have come this far in *The Dragon's Touch* and not skipped a page, then you have taken the first step to learning. You have ventured into the beliefs and teachings of an art form inconsistent with those taught in martial arts schools. Now take the time to study *The Dragon's Touch*, learn, absorb, practice. Become the Dragon, live the Dragon, practice the Dragon. Train hard, apply yourself to the study, apply your study to practice, apply your practice only when your actions are just and true. For as the Dragon lives within the soul of a true martial artist, there also lives the Universal Force. Be its champion, not its victim.

May you live in peace.